MW00628582

# TITANIC Jessie and Lifeboat #9

# TITANIC Jessie and Lifeboat #9

## The Untold Story

Kelley Bortner

Kelley Senkowski

# CONTENTS

# CONTENTS

First Printing, 2023

This book is written for, and on behalf of, my children, and all of the family and descendants of Jessie.
This is for you all.

A special thank you and love to my husband, children, and friends who encouraged me; to my sister, for her partnership in all of the research; my daughter for helping with edits; and to extended family for any information that was provided as passed down from Jessie. Thank you to God, the Father, for giving me the story and the purpose to write it down.

**May Jessie's story not be lost to the depths of history...**

*"However, I consider my life worth nothing to me:
my only aim is to finish the race and complete the task
the Lord Jesus has given me -
the task of testifying to the good news of God's grace."*

*Acts 20:24 NIV*

# Introduction

In the early 1900s, with the turn of the century came a shift in American culture, from horse and buggy to car both occupying the road simultaneously. Women slowly began to be more visible with their employment and transitioned from big dresses to more stream-lined styles with large day hats for upper-class women.

World travel by ships was becoming more commonplace with transatlantic travel open to all. Luxury and opulence were in high demand by those with the means to pay for it. As new hotels were built, they were grand, with gilded trim, expensive artwork, and the best food, dishes, and linens, as was the expectation.

Based on the high demand for opulence, a ship was being designed on the other side of the world with a level of opulence, luxury, and comfort never before achieved on a ship. The ship touted top-of-the-line linens, dishes, flatware, collectible artwork, and gilded trim. To ensure the safety of this almost priceless opulence, an innovative design for the structure of the ship was being used to guarantee the investment was safe in an *unsinkable* ship. It was to be named the Titanic, due to its sheer size, which was unparalleled at the time.

The promotion, hype, and excitement generated around this phenomenal ship were unprecedented around the world. World-class athletes, movie stars, business gurus topping the wealthiest in the world, and movie celebrities booked cabins on this extravagant liner. First-class suites ran the length of the ship with multiple rooms. Second-class accommodations mirrored first-class cabin size and dining opulence on any other ship of the time. Third-class rooms mirrored second-class accommodations on other ships and were to be filled with immigrant families and young adults who used their life's savings to travel, dreaming of a new future in America.

There were newspaper stories, postcards, coins, and stamps circulating in cities around the globe featuring the Titanic. People bought tickets a year in advance to be on the maiden voyage of the already famous ship.

This is the world that Laura Ingles Wilder's daughter, Rose, was growing up in and becoming an independent woman. At that time, while Rose was growing up, so was a young lady across the ocean in Scotland, named Jessie.

# 1

## Highlands of My Heart

*Aberdeenshire, East coast of Scotland - April 1904*

Jessie woke to the patter of light rain on the roof above her bed. The fresh smells of new rain always brought a warm feeling of home in the Highlands, and she lingered just a moment longer to savor the memory for the many days ahead. She quickly dressed and woke her younger siblings to begin getting ready for the day's journey. There were daily chores to be finished before breakfast, rain or shine, although the absence of farm chores that day was replaced with last-minute packing.

Jessie's father, George Bruce ran a successful cattle breeding farm in Aberdeenshire, Scotland, to support his wife, Mary Ann Booth Bruce, and their eleven children. Yet, things had become more difficult in the cattle breeding business in Scotland, as the country was landlocked by the sea. To continue his cattle breeding George felt the need to move to a location with more land, which allowed him the opportunity to increase cattle. Scotland, being surrounded by the ocean, was saturated with other breeders. He had tried buying land from multiple sources unsuccessfully, and because there was no more good grazing land unclaimed on the large island, he was forced to look elsewhere. George had heard stories of endless land waiting to be claimed or given away in America, so there would be cattle farms in need of breeders. This opportunity sounded nothing short of a dream; a dream for cattle breeding, and especially for his family. He set in place a plan to relocate his farm and family.

As one of the oldest of eleven children, at eighteen years old, Jessie spent much of her day caring for the younger children in the house and assisting her mother with the household chores and schooling. She felt her nerves this morning all along her small frame of four feet, nine inches tall. She felt physical pain knowing her youngest siblings would not remember the lush, rolling highland hills and the fresh smell of earth and heather whenever it rained, or the tang of the sea. Scotland was home.

Mary Ann (Booth) and George Bruce in later years
*Kelley Senkowski / no use without permission*

The knot in the pit of her stomach had been building over the last couple of weeks, and today was the day that she and her family would leave her beautiful, beloved Scotland behind, from the deck of a ship, as she watched it grow smaller, along with her sense of home.

She was a Bruce, of the clan of Robert the Bruce from long ago, and she drew strength, recalling the clan motto, FUIMUS, *We Have Been*, as she would leave Scotland for an unknown future.

As she helped finish feeding her family with what items were not yet packed for breakfast use, Jessie set her strong-lined jaw, held her head up, tamped down the nerves in her stomach, and began the final packing of last-minute items. Her mind wandered as she went about her tasks. She knew this day would change her life forever, as she sailed to a new land, new people, and new smells when it rained.

She had always thought that she would one day marry a Highlander and build a home not far from her parents and siblings. Now, she wondered what her future would hold. She had just reached the age considered very eligible for marriage and knew that the few young men in the area that she had thought might court her now would not have the opportunity and she must put them out of her mind.

Her oldest sister, Maggie, had just been married a few weeks earlier and was starting her new life in Scotland with her husband, Alexander. Her other older sibling, Georgina, had been working as a domestic help since she was twelve years old for a nice family not far from her parents. She had met a nice gentleman, George, a blacksmith for machine parts, and married him three years ago and they had an infant son, little Georgie. Her married sisters and her grandparents were staying in Scotland. She knew her father could not have been thinking of her marriage prospects in making his decision to move a very large family and business to a land of more opportunity, as he had to consider the many mouths that needed feeding. But Jessie considered it.

The cattle breeding business that he ran kept him busy much of the time, and Jessie was aware of the mounting tension between her parents as they discussed the slowing business. A new and emerging country would mean endless land in which to breed and run a cattle business which would indeed help the family. With thoughts of a new land, Jessie resigned herself to a future of helping her family and caring for her younger siblings. She knew her mother needed help and she loved her family life. Still, her bright blue eyes glistened, and she swallowed the lump that formed in thinking she would not hold her own children anytime soon. She felt off balance suddenly, as if her equilibrium were off, just thinking about it.

As she collected herself, she sent her brother, eleven-year-old John, out with another bundle to pack, and she heard her father call to the family that it was time to leave.

"Coming!" she called out as she scooped up her little, three-year-old sister, Lottie, in one arm and a basket of food for the midday meal in the other. As one pair of young, questioning eyes looked into her intelligent eyes, she could see the anxiousness in her sweet, little sister, Lottie's, face.

"It will be alright. I'm with you. I'll keep you warm, wee cherub. It'll be a fun adventure!" she whispered close to Lottie.

With one long look around her secure, lovely home to keep the memory forever, she left to join her waiting family in the wagon.

She felt her mother's comforting arm encircle her shoulders as she fell in step beside her. Mother held two-year-old, Dora, on her opposite hip. Jessie handed Lottie into the arms of her thirteen-year-old brother, Alexander, in the wagon and turned to her grandparents to give them a quick, tear-filled hug and say goodbye. Her family wasn't much for showing emotion, but this was a rare time that called for an embrace, not knowing when or if there would ever be another. Her grandparents had always been there, through everything in her life, every new sibling and skinned knee. She would miss her grandparents terribly. Her two older sisters had come to say their goodbyes to the family also, and she gave them each a silent, tear-streaked hug, and joined the family in the wagon.

As they rode to the port, she looked around at the faces of her younger sisters and brothers and gave them a shaky, yet sincere smile of reassurance. She thought of her older sisters, married and living their own life in Scotland.

*When would she see them again?*

Whatever lay ahead, she, and those next to her at that moment, would journey together as a family. All eight siblings by her side were making the move with her, and her parents. That gave her comfort.

As they neared the docks the bustle of ship loading and hurrying people was a bit overwhelming compared to the quiet nature of the farm left behind. At the docks, she ushered her siblings to a tree next to the road, and she and her sister, Mimi, three years younger, handed out some cheese, apples, and hard bread to their family members for the midday meal. She was glad that they would not be setting sail on an empty stomach.

As they ate their meal, her father and brother, Alexander, made the last arrangements for boarding the belongings that they brought along. The rest of the luggage had been sent ahead, and the cattle sold. Her father planned to find new stock when they reached their next home location.

The Allan Liner RMS *Corinthian* looked very intimidating as she gazed up at the ship that would be their home for a time. Her mind seemed to go blank with the chaos of preparing a ship to set sail that swarmed all around her. All of the older children had the hand of a younger one as they huddled together in hopes of not getting knocked out of the way by the bustle. Jessie could smell horses, mixed with the familiar scent of the sea, and she heard the jingle of passing wagons followed by the putt of an occasional car. She heard people shouting or talking nearby as she struggled to take in all the sights and sounds at once.

"Mother, remind me in what port we will arrive?" Jessie inquired to her mother above the heads of the little ones. Her mother looked at her questioning blue eyes, as the wind blew light tendrils around Jessie's head.

"We will sail into Canada - Rockland, Ontario to be precise - for a time to adjust. Then we will travel to the States when your father is ready, to find a place to settle", Mother stated, trying to sound confident of her husband's plans.

Just hearing her repeat the plans seemed to give confidence to the older children for the journey ahead, including Jessie.

She noticed a newspaper herald on the docks as they waited, announcing details of the Olympic Games to start soon, which reminded her of their good fortune. The upcoming Olympic Games were being held in the country of their final destination, not far from Canada, in a place called St. Louis, Missouri, so securing passage close to the event must not have been easy for her father. With her older sisters not being present, they were a party of eleven, plus the accompaniment of luggage with which to start their new home.

Her father, George, waved from across the street for his family to join him. With a flutter in her stomach, excitement, or nerves she wasn't sure - maybe both - Jessie and her sister, Nellie, younger than her by one year, helped her mother lead the large family group over to their father. Then they all made their way onto the ship to get settled. The *Corinthian* would take them all to Canada, where they would make their way to America.

The days at sea passed by quickly with caring for the younger family members who were confined to a ship for days on end. The frigid wind kept them inside more than outside. Without much opportunity to meet other passengers, they had arrived in Canada before Jessie knew it. Her father had written in advance to secure a home large enough for their family and they would stay there for a time while he made final preparations for the move to America. It would take time and multiple trips for him and her brothers to journey back and forth, find a breeder's job at a farm with plentiful land, and a homestead, and then move them all. Ontario would be home for the family in the meantime.

Having never been out of Scotland before, at eighteen years old, she felt like a child in a strange land. Although the people spoke English as she did, it was so different, and there were many new and unfamiliar words, so Jessie struggled to understand shopkeepers and others, and they to understand her brogue. She thought that it would be a blessing that her youngest siblings would grow up with less of the Scottish brogue and a more Western sound to their speech.

The family found a place that housed them all, went about the daily activities trying to make the best of their situation, and kept as much to their family's normal routine as possible. They all knew they were not permanently staying there, but what they didn't know was how long it would be.

# 2

# A New Life

Jessie woke, looked over at her sister nearest to her, Dora, still fast asleep with the sweet expression of sleepy youth, and heard the rhythmic patter of light rain outside. She had the same feeling of anticipation and nervousness she had seven years ago when she listened to the rain in the Highlands on the morning of their departure from Scotland. Although not as vividly as she once did, she could almost smell the Highland fresh smells of grass and heather when she closed her eyes, and she smiled. It was March 28, 1911 - her wedding day!

Thinking of the Highlands again gave her mixed emotions as she thought of her grandparents and older sister, and their absence on her wedding day.

Jessie was so excited and grateful that her other sister, Georgina, and her family, had moved here recently and lived nearby in town. Georgina's family had not been happy with a move to Dublin, Ireland, so Jessie's parents helped them all immigrate to the States recently to be near them.

Her other older sister, Maggie, and her family had immigrated to Minnesota three years ago but weren't able to travel for the wedding.

She and William could pay them a visit in the near future so they could meet her husband. Jessie was happy one of her older sisters could attend, along with the rest of the family.

Jessie felt a small knot in her stomach as she thought about this being her last morning attending to her family. Yet, she felt a quick thrill run through her, followed by a tinge of nerves as her next thought was of William. This would also be her wedding night and the beginning of her life with her beloved William. *William.* Jessie thought. *My heart.*

William Henry Trout, the son of Oscar Trout, of Columbus, Ohio, was a widower. He had one of the sought-after jobs of the working class at the time, as a switchman, working for the Hockings Valley Railroad, at the Mound Street Railyard. She would be *Mrs. Jessie Laird Trout* by the end of the day. Jessie, now 25 years old, loved William with all of her heart, and she felt he was worth the wait!

Thinking back to the almost five years since they arrived in America seemed like a blur. They felt so out-of-sorts at first, everything was so different; from food and smells, to customs, clothes, and even the sound of language and the words themselves. When Jessie was 21 years old, her father, George, brought his family into the States through White Bear Lake, Minnesota, and they journeyed to Columbus, Ohio, where he settled his family and began rebuilding his cattle breeding business. Jessie stayed behind with her brother to finish the last of the packing at the rental home the family had shared. They traveled through Detroit in 1906 a few days before Christmas and made their way to join the family in Ohio.

In their new home, the neighbors, although a distance away, were friendly and she and her siblings soon fell into a new routine of tending house, school, and helping their father. The little ones were all growing up so quickly and many even sounded more American lately than Scottish. Jessie was thinking back a few months ago to when she met William, as she finished the morning dishes and shooed the last of the youngsters out the door. Mama was in the other room sewing clothing repairs with items piled next to her waiting their turn. Jessie reminisced to herself about the whirlwind courting and her time with William as she absently performed morning house tasks that she had done so many times before.

+ + +

*4 months earlier*

After almost five years of being settled in Columbus, the days for Jessie were a routine of food preparation before sunrise, cleaning before schooling the young ones, and assisting her father outside on the endless house and business chores when she had the time.

Jessie and her sister walked through town one day to mail a letter to her sister Maggie, who lived with her husband Alexander, and her young son, Edward, in Minnesota. As they neared the post office, Jessie saw a group of men, who, from their attire, seemed to be off for the day from working in the railyard nearby on Mound Street. That wasn't unusual, with so many workers at the railyard there were groups often in town, yet this time, one seemed to beckon her regard. She felt a jolt of energy when he caught her eye the one moment she glanced up. She was startled as she looked away, having never felt such a sensation before, which caused her to stumble up the steps of the post office.

Her sister three years younger, Mimi, was beside her and noticed the whole unusual happening, realizing that the cause was not from the random early snow pile on the street, and sent a teasing comment in her direction.

*This is ridiculous!* Jessie mentally scolded herself. *25 is way past the age for blushing!*

She said as much in response to Mimi's comment as she walked through the door of the establishment. Yet, she couldn't help but glance around as she exited the building, in complete fear that he would still be in sight, and hoping he would.

*What was that?* she wondered.

She still felt shaky for the next few hours just from the electric glance of his eyes and her confusing reaction. She pondered the event that night as she fell asleep, and her ridiculous reaction. She knew there was no hope for a husband at her age. Jessie was used to preparing her sisters for their suiters to call on them and the men's preference for a younger lady in choosing a wife. Yet, she had never felt that jolt before, from a mere man, or anything else! What was it about him? He was tall and lean, yet muscular, but so were many other men who she encountered without incident weekly. He was a handsome man - not a boy, and she was an older woman, with a strong jaw and lips too full. She convinced herself that it was just a random glance on his part, probably done often with any woman he encountered, with no effect on him, *only on her.*

+ + +

A few days later, it was a blustery late fall day and Jessie and a few of her siblings headed into town on errands for her mother. An early snow had fallen for the season, but most had melted already. There must have been a political or social event nearby because the streets were unusually busy with wagons and horses, and a few cars interspersed. There were moments when one could barely see to the other side of the street and the buzz of the crowd was constant. She didn't follow events that went on in town, yet she was sure she would hear bits of information just walking on the street regarding the extra crowds. Jessie, her sisters, and her brother, carefully chose a clear moment to make their way across to the other side of the street.

Suddenly, a pair of strong hands grabbed her around the shoulders as she instinctively reached for her younger siblings who were just behind her moments ago. She was halfway across the street and as a horse and buggy passed, another unseen one came from the opposite direction just as she was stepping out to make her way across to the other street side.

Her startled light blue eyes looked up into eyes that seemed to sizzle to her core with a burst of energy. She recognized him as the man she had seen weeks earlier in town at a glance that seared her memory. He stood holding her shoulders, facing her, and looking into her eyes for what seemed like an inappropriate amount of time.

He seemed to shake out of it, dropped his hands, and in a smooth, deep voice, said, "Pardon me, ma'am, you were in danger of getting struck". He immediately bade his excuses at the sound of, "William! Catch up, gotta go!", by his friends, and continued his walk across to the street side she had just left.

Her eleven-year-old, younger sister, Lottie, was now pulling her forcefully to get across to safety, as Jessie looked back over her shoulder in stunned confusion. Her sisters and brother were excitedly talking about their near accident and checking that no one was hurt. Her whole body seemed to be trembling, and it wasn't only because of the near collision with a horse and buggy.

All Jessie heard was buzzing in her ears as she glanced back down the other side of the street to see William look back and nod at her as he joined his companions and walked further on.

*William is his name. Of course, it is,* she reflected. As she relived the past moments to herself, she thought he seemed to hold her direct gaze and shoulders longer than necessary, and differently than someone who just bumped into another person unexpectedly.

*Could he also feel the energy of their contact? Was it her imagination? Or, worse, did he notice she acted inappropriately? She must stop her musing,* she mentally scolded herself and shook it off. *It is only going to cause misplaced hope.*

+ + +

The following week her father needed her to go into town with him and she silently berated herself for looking for those warm eyes from the previous near collision in the street. She went to the general store with a list from her mother while her father visited the blacksmith. She would meet her father at the wagon after their errands.

Suddenly, as she searched a shelf of items for what her mother needed, William appeared near her side with a soft greeting. She was so surprised she turned wide-eyed with her mouth agape until she recovered herself enough to return a greeting in kind. William asked for her name, and introduced himself, then began an easy conversation with her. She soon was giggling at something he said and mentally checking herself for behaving like a schoolgirl, but his kind and easy humor caught her off guard.

She lost track of time while they chatted until she saw her father walk by the store window towards the wagon. She excused herself from William to finish her mother's list and meet her father at the wagon as quickly as she could. She already knew she would hear about it taking too long from her father.

William was not to be daunted, and offered to wait for her to complete her shop so he could assist her in carrying her purchases to the wagon. She explained that it wasn't necessary, fearing her father would be there before her, but William kindly restated his intention.

Assisting her in carrying the bags afforded William the opportunity he needed to introduce himself to her father and ask for permission to stop over to see her, which he proceeded to do.

On the drive back home with her father, she felt like her face was burning coal, yet she felt nicely warm all over as she thought back over the sweet, chance meeting. She had never met a man she could easily talk to, and that left her confused and happy. She was used to the no-nonsense way of her father and Grandfather growing up in Scotland. William - his way, his voice, and his interest in *her*, was a sweet, refreshing warm cup of tea in her world. She was trembling with excitement that he may call upon her and that he had the courage to approach her father for permission to do so.

He did stop over to visit the next day, and after that was a rose-colored, honey-sweet blur of quiet walks, lots of laughs, picnics together bundled against the chill wind, holding hands, and dinner with her family. Soon a marriage proposal followed.

Just thinking back to the whirlwind of it, the longing for his company and the sound of his voice when they were apart, made her head spin and brought a brilliant smile to her face. Just then, Dora awoke and saw Jessie's brilliant smile as she reminisced, and said, "It's your wedding day! Let's get you ready!"

+ + +

She was marrying William today, and she could barely catch her breath over that fact. He was a quiet, polite, and sincere man to everyone with whom he came in contact. To her, he whispered his life's dreams, endearing affection, and engaged in intelligent conversations with her, while respecting her thoughts and dreams. He was well worth the wait, and she thanked God for such a gift and a blessing to her. Having William in her life made every day exciting to wake up to, and she adored him.

That day was a little gray with sprinkles, but Jessie didn't notice. She was walking in a ray of sunshine today. She was dressed and ready to head to the church early, as her mother walked into her room. Her sisters had been gathered and assisting Jessie with her hair and preparations and exited once Mother walked in, sensing the moment.

"I'm very happy for you, Jessie. He's a good man," stated her mother, looking into Jessie's eyes, then added, "You look radiant." Jessie was almost giddy as she felt a rush of excitement at her mother's words. And then the nerves hit, and she teared up.

"Thank you, Mother. He makes me very happy" responded Jessie. "I have waited for this day all of my life, yet a part of me is grieving leaving you and my sisters and brothers, and you with all of the household responsibilities," Jessie explained while looking down as she fidgeted her hands.

Mother gently lifted her chin so that their eyes met. "My Jess, you have been a blessing to our family all of these years, and now it is time for your own family. We will be fine. We have lots of hands to help", answered her mother with a sheen of tears in her eyes.

Just then, they turned their heads toward the stairs as they heard her teen brother, Robert, a floor below, announce the arrival of the carriage to take her to the church where she would begin a new life with her beloved, William.

# 3

## Golden Days and a Bleeding Heart

William was a widower, so he already had a house at 1284 ½ Broad Street in Columbus, Ohio. Jessie had only been to his house a couple of times previously, with a sibling as a chaperone, to visit or bring a meal to William. It was in town not far from the railyard for William to walk to work each morning, and Jessie was excited to make it a home for the two of them.

The days and weeks after the wedding of William and Jessie had been like heaven for her. She enjoyed talking and laughing with him as they went about the household tasks, and she loved setting up the house to be their new home. The nights were amazing, as they held each other close nestled under the blanket, and talked of the children they wanted, and of their childhoods. Jessie talked endlessly about Scotland to him, knowing it was a replacement for him to see it himself.

Jessie's parents lived at a ranch, known as the Johnson Farm, which was just outside of town, so in fair weather when she was up for a long walk, she could walk part of the way and pay a wagon for a ride the rest of the distance, to help her mother. Today was one of those days. As she packed up what she needed for the day to help her mother with chores and assist her younger siblings, she grabbed a canteen and apple as she looked around her quaint home. She loved her three-bedroom home with the little backyard where she and William loved to catch up on the day after dinner, holding hands on the swing and talking about the world news, his work, the day happenings, and dreaming of a future where the house would be filled with their littles. As she gave a last glance around and shut the door, she thought, *the little house with giant dreams.*

She adored Spring's newness after a cold winter, with fresh smells and the warm sun on her face. It seemed the perfect time for her and William to start their new life together, she thought with a smile that softened her strong jawline and her blue eyes. The road was busy with the day's happenings, and the jingle of horses and wagons mixed with an occasional car moving slowly as it softly chugged by. There was a slight breeze today that brought sweet smells of lilacs and early blooming peonies as she passed by the last houses on the main street near where she would catch a ride the rest of the way.

Soon, along the wagon ride the houses were sparser and she inhaled deeply of the fragrant air of the country and smells of grasses and soil overturned from recent planting. It reminded her of the beauty and scents of beloved Scotland. She longed to go back some-day, and she hoped to share it with William. She sighed as she already missed him and couldn't wait to be near him this evening at the end of his workday. He worked long hours, and she looked forward to time with him after his work shift came to an end.

The wagon dropped her off and she walked up the long drive to the ranch where her parents lived. Her father had built up a cattle breeding ranch again and the scents of farm and cattle were familiar. She walked into the house to the smell of baking bread and several siblings milling around. After greeting them, and her mom calling the stranglers to the main room for schooling and chores, she got to work on their education. Jessie felt it was so good to be surrounded by a large family again, sometimes it was too quiet with just the two of them at home. Her mother must have caught the same thought as she looked over at Jessie from the kitchen with an inquiring look.

Intelligent eyes met each other over the children, and Jessie gave a slight shake of her head with a gentle smile to her mother, who smiled back and went back to her kitchen tasks. Her mother would be so excited to have a new baby around again, after raising 11 of her own, who were then mostly adults and the rest school age.

Jessie was so very happy and excited to see what the future held for her. She suddenly wanted to write to her older sister, Maggie in Minnesota, as she often did, and share more of daily life with her.

+ + +

Spring turned into the hazy days of summer, and she came to her parents less often while the kids took a break from schooling and helped their father with summer chores. When she visited, there were days of helping her mother, sipping lemonade in the shade of a huge oak tree out back for a cooling break from the heat and humidity. Some days William came to join the family for dinner after his shift at the railyard.

Summer turned into fall, with cooler evenings, while the colors of the trees along the main street began to show hints of turning into a glorious riot of gold and red.

## September 22, 1911

Jessie was watering her garden out back and had just come in to grab a knife for cutting some flowers when she heard a knock at the door. Her mind was on Mr. & Mrs. Trout coming for dinner that evening, as William's parents lived nearby. She quickly emptied her hands, wiped them absently on her apron, and opened the door.

Later, all that she remembered of that moment were the two somberly dressed, serious gentlemen and the look on their faces. The next moment she remembered was sitting on the floor repeating William's name over and over, as her heart and dreams seemed shattered all around her on the floor.

Her sister, Nellie, was standing over her trying to get her up onto the sofa with gentle, coaxing words. She had come to help Jessie with dinner prep for that evening and had walked in behind the men.

ca. 1912 Locomotive Baltimore and Ohio
*National Parks Gallery - Public Use*

The next memory she had was waking up in bed and her mother leaning over her with a soft greeting. Nellie, was nearby in the room and, joining them at the bedside, her mother and sister put the pieces together for Jessie.

She had a hard time grasping their words and felt like her mind was in a fog with everything slowed down. William had been in a horrific accident at the Mound Street Railyard, or viaduct, while working as a switchman, and was hit by a train and then run over immediately afterward. He died instantly and they wouldn't allow her to see him.

*This isn't real,* she thought. *Their wedding had been just six months earlier, they had dreams, wanted to have lots of children, this cannot be real! There must be a mistake.*

Jessie was devastated and did not have the energy to get out of bed, except to walk through the burial tasks laying him to rest at the Greenlawn cemetery. It had been a closed casket, and she would never look into his eyes again, with the last time being fleeting as he said goodbye in the dark of morning and headed to work days ago.

She was constantly wearing the beautiful hair combs and bracelet that William had given her for their wedding, only taking them off when she was able to crawl back in bed anytime she had the opportunity. Nellie stayed with her the first few nights, but Jessie could not bear to sleep in the bed that still smelled of William and to look around at everything they created together in the house, with dreams of their future lives. Jessie was utterly devastated and said that she didn't want to live without her William.

She held out hope that some part of him would remain with her in the form of a baby, but with the stress, a couple of days after his death she realized that was also taken away from her as the normal course of life returned to her body on schedule. She was sobbing on the floor and feeling like a puddle after a storm when the realization hit her that there would not be anything of William again.

Nellie held Jessie close, rocking and whispering, "I'm so sorry, Things are going to get better."

But she thought Jessie would be better if not left alone at this time and should go stay at their parents' home temporarily.

Nellie talked to her family, and they let Jessie know that they intended to move her to the ranch. Jessie didn't have much reaction as she somehow seemed a hollow version of the person she had been. She was moved from her Broad Street home into her parents' home so they could care for her and help her get back on her feet.

Five weeks later, Jessie turned 26 years old. She seemed lost and struggled with depression, not able to find herself or her place any longer. She was functioning now and assisting with chores and the children, but her spark was gone, and her eyes were empty. She continued to sleep when she wasn't helping the family. Her birthday seemed to signal to her parents that Jessie needed to move on in life and they began talking with her about her immediate and future plans.

It was difficult for Jessie, but she knew she could not stay a burden to her parents as another mouth to feed, and she had no desire to find another husband. She was too old to live at home, no longer a wife, too young to be without a love, and struggling with why she was the one alive instead of her beloved William.

By sheer strength of will, she formulated a plan. She would sell her house on Broad Street, as she couldn't bear to be there and see William in the porch planks that he fixed, in the garden that he framed for her, the emptiness of the children they would never have, in the bedroom that was a paradise retreat for them after long days of work and supper at the kitchen table.

*No. She must sell the house to ever move on, one day at a time,* she determined.

She could give her parents some money to put towards the farm to help offset the expenses of another mouth to feed. Where she would settle after that, she didn't yet know.

# 4

## Grey Days and Bright Adventures

As the last of the glorious fall colors of the trees blew away in the breeze, Jessie was cleaning out the remaining items that she would take from the Broad Street house and loading them in the wagon on the street outside. The furniture that her mother or siblings didn't want would be sold with the house.

Just then, an eager, smiling gentleman approached her at the wagon as she turned from loading her last personal items. The gentleman removed his hat and inquired if she was Jessie Trout.

After pleasantries were exchanged, he handed her an envelope, explaining that the railroad company sent her a letter with a sizable pension for her husband's unfortunate fatal accident. She blinked, wiped her hands on her apron, and felt for her hair, that it was staying where she had pinned it, then took the envelope from his waiting, outstretched hand.

"Pardon me? I am not expecting a letter," she stated as she took it.

He seemed to be waiting expectantly so she opened it to look inside. It was a banknote, and her eyes met his, showing her complete surprise. It was substantial and would be a great help to her as a 26-year-old, very single, woman. She didn't know how to grasp this surprise and absently stared at the banknote as the gentleman excused himself. She stood there for some time trying to process what had just happened, and then tucked it away in her handbag. She would need some time to process this surprise development.

A few weeks went by and as Christmas preparations began with much to do in the coming days, Jessie tried to muster some sliver of joy in her days, as she stayed with her parents. She helped them as best she could with the house and farm chores, trying to imagine her next step in life, and what the money meant for her future, but it seemed too hard to imagine anything at this point. Fall had turned into winter, summer chores were long past, and schooling and assisting her siblings was a regular task again, whenever her mother didn't need her help.

She hadn't cashed the banknote yet as she didn't have any interest in doing that or anything else. She didn't have much interest in social events, and as a single woman in 1911, she wasn't allowed to do much on her own, travel required a chaperone in some places, and taking care of a home all by herself was not an option. Work for women was just beginning to be acceptable in special instances.

She couldn't shake the cloud of grief after three months and decided she would use the pension to travel back to her beloved Scotland to visit her grandparents again and maybe she could figure out a path for her future while surrounded by the familiar greenery and scents of the Highlands.

She sat down to write to her grandparents about her plan for an upcoming visit, she had missed them terribly. Her only regret was that her grandparents, and her sister Maggie in Minnesota, had never met her beloved William. She last saw her grandparents as a girl, and now, she was returning to them as a widow. Jessie shook herself, pushed to keep moving, and began the letter.

+ + +

With the railyard pension, Jessie was able to purchase a round-trip first-class ticket for herself, on the White Star Line's large ship, the *Oceanic*, scheduled to set sail on January 12, 1912. The ship was one of the largest afloat and said to be luxurious. It would be very different from the ship that she, and all of her siblings, sailed on with her parents years ago.

*This was scary and very exhilarating,* she thought. For the first time in many months, there was a glimmer of light that cracked through the gloom for Jessie, along with shaky nerves.

She had decided to travel in first class since she was traveling alone and a new wardrobe was a necessity for the trip. She was used to living in a town and helping on a farm and did not have the proper attire. She used more of the pension dollars and paid a visit to a tailor in town. In addition to the many dresses for day and evening, and several shoes for different occasions, she would need a new warm coat for winter, a hat, and gloves, as it would be cold on deck in January. She was excited to get a wardrobe in the newest, straight-cut skirts of the day, as no more bustle and flair of her childhood was worn. She would need hats for the day dresses, and she was relieved that no headwear was required in the evening for ladies' formal wear.

The holidays for Jessie were a blur of activity, bustle, helping her mother, tailoring appointments with her sister's company, and packing.

A couple weeks before departure, Jessie was with her older sister, Georgina, and her family, headed to the home of a photographer so they could take a rare picture of them all together. Jessie needed a photo to add to her passport so she thought she could get one from the photographer at this time as well.

She relished the children's chatter and soaked in the moments as they walked along the streets of Columbus. Jessie enjoyed the outing as she listened to the easy conversation of the parents, and the giggles and protests of the children as they walked along the street in the blustery, damp early winter day.

Jessie was excited to be wearing her new warm coat, and hat that she had purchased for her first-class trip.

She carried Maggie's youngest child as they walked the last couple of houses and struggled to keep a grip on little Jimmy with all of the layers that an infant wears in the cold, damp weather. She smiled to herself, thinking it was like trying to carry a heavy, large squirming pillow, while she listened to the chatter of the children.

Jessie (center) with sister Margaret and family -
passport photo for Jessie
*Kelley Senkowski / no use without permission*

+ + +

Soon, it was time to start her journey! Jessie felt a mix of emotions that broke through the haze of depression that came and went.

She grieved, feeling she was leaving William in her heart, yet again, along with her parents and siblings. She also felt nervous, excited for adventure on her own for the first time in her life, and eager for a return to Scotland.

The thought of traveling and being independent was the most thrilling and fearful thought she had, and completely foreign to her. Saying goodbye to her parents and siblings to leave on her own would be difficult for Jessie, as she felt she would return a different person somehow.

+ + +

## January 1912

Jessie waited in line with her arms full of bags she wanted kept close, until it was her turn in line to board the White Star Line, *Oceanic*. The rest of her larger luggage was being loaded with the first-class, or Saloon, porters.

The *Oceanic* looked massive as she peered up at the sight above her. She had heard that there would be over 1700 people aboard!

White Star Line, R.M.S Oceanic
*Wikipedia / Public Use*

It was a transatlantic ocean liner, with two massive stacks that were yellow orange in color. The stacks were in a shade she hadn't quite seen before outside of nature, almost the color of fall leaves. It had been the largest ship in the world, until shortly before she moved from Scotland years ago, with ships being built even larger in 1912.

There were crowds around the ship waiting to wave goodbye for the send-off of whatever loved one was onboard. Her father made sure she arrived safely at the port but as she stood in line alone, she felt the weight of her decision to travel solo, and she felt small. Being a part of a family of 11 children and then being married, she had never had any occasion to be alone for any length of time.

It was liberating as much as it was frightening. Her being alone and of small stature made it easy to get overlooked in a crowd and she had to keep alert at all times so as not to miss her turn or cue from the ship personnel.

She was grateful for the newly purchased long coat she had acquired as part of her travel attire and hugged it closer against the chill gusts of sea wind at the dock. She breathed in the salty ocean air and couldn't wait to be back on Scottish soil, where the smell of the sea was never far away. Being in Columbus, she had missed the familiar smell of the ocean.

It was finally her turn to board and she was impressed by the details of the woodwork, paneling, and the lights of first-class accommodations, as she walked the corridors to her appointed cabin.

There was a very comfortable and spacious library, or Saloon, with detailed wooden paneling for first-class passengers to have a place to sit and mingle after a meal.

Her cabin was pleasant, yet it felt strange to her to be in it alone. She immediately sat on the bed after the flurry of activity of the morning and it was comfortable. She looked around her cabin for a few moments getting acquainted with her temporary home, then unpacked a few items before heading to the deck to wave to the bystanders crowded on the dock watching the ship depart.

After she shuffled and squeezed to get a view, feeling the cold wind in her face was exhilarating! As the ship departed the docks a little while later, she turned her attention to what she would wear to dress for dinner in the first-class dining room.

This was already an amazing experience, and she was looking forward to meeting other passengers at dinner. Maybe she would find some other lady companions for the trip, as she had no interest in meeting men.

The meals on board were flavorful. Jessie would tag along to walk to meals with other ladies on her floor, but she didn't get to know them well. She was quiet but smiled and answered when spoken to, yet she felt very vulnerable for her first experience alone. It took a few days to get used to thinking only of herself when deciding when to get up, when to go to bed, where to go around the ship, and what to do to pass the hours of sailing.

She was slowly exhaling and relaxing after the flurry and blur of the past months. By the time she departed the ship, she was walking a little more confidently and felt a small sense of freedom.

# 5

## Heather and Sea

It was warming slightly in Scotland with early spring arriving. The smells, early blooms, and greenery were breathtaking to Jessie, and she never tired of them. Not being too far inland from the coast, the sea air was crisp and refreshing.

She felt the healing hand of God upon her as she sat in and gazed at the Highland terrain, and went for walks on familiar trails from her childhood when granted free moments between chores helping her grandparents.

However, she had forgotten how little sun there was in the Highlands, after having been in the States for eight years, this was a surprise realization.

Aberdeenshire, Scotland, UK
*Suzanne Neumann / Getty Images*

The trip over had been very nice, yet somewhat lonely traveling alone for the first time. When she traveled by ship to the States all those years ago, she had been surrounded by her very large family.

People were pleasant enough and first-class accommodations were beautiful and very comfortable on the *Oceanic*. Since Jessie was a bit subdued she didn't make any lasting friendships but enjoyed her sailing.

When she arrived in Scotland, it was so nice to see her grandparents and visit with them, but Jessie was feeling restless after a time as early spring arrived, and she decided to leave sooner than she planned, to go visit her sister in London before departing back home.

Maggie was in London, with her husband, Alex, and son Edward, for a visit and she could stay with them before departure. She could take the ship back from a port there instead of returning to the States from Scotland.

She had missed Margaret deeply and they had been exchanging letters while she was visiting her grandparents in Scotland. Maggie had invited her to visit London while she was in the same part of the world.

For her return home, Jessie could depart for her parent's home from Southampton, near London, in early April on the same ship, the *Oceanic,* instead of the port in Scotland.

She thought, *God is good,* as she secured her plans for the London visit to see Maggie.

She must be healing as she was beginning to sorely miss her family back home and felt the pull to begin her future in the States, whatever that held for her.

+ + +

*March 1912*

As the date that would have been her first wedding anniversary neared, Jessie said goodbye to the beloved hills of green and heather that was Scotland, and to her grandparents. In mid-March, she traveled to England by ship and then rode the Boat Train to London. She stayed at the home where Maggie and her family were staying, and after they picked her up from the train station, she was surrounded by family once again. Jessie had always had many young siblings around her, had missed it, and very much enjoyed getting to know her nephew who was nine years old.

Jessie spent lovely days with Maggie over tea, helping her around the house and catching up on many years since their last visit. Jessie felt it was so good to see her! They talked of growing up in Scotland and running in the hills, the beach walks before there were so many little Bruces running around, then how the family grew, school, holiday parties with the neighbors, and what the future may now hold for Jessie.

"How are you, really, my sister?" said Maggie over tea and short-bread one day.

Jessie's eyes teared up a bit and she blinked back the tears. It was the day of her and William's wedding anniversary.

She responded, "I'm much better than I have been. I just wish William and you had met, as it feels like he never was at times, with some family members not having met him."

Jessie paused a moment the then added quietly, "But, I am ready to figure out my future when I get home. I can't live with our parents forever and I'm not looking for a husband. There are some jobs for women now, maybe I'll explore that option."

Her sister reached over and squeezed her hand with a smile and understanding eyes, but added no comment.

+ + +

It was a cold day with drizzle at the end of March and Jessie, Margaret, and Alex, ventured out to the streets to run errands before the midday meal. Jessie had worn her warmest coat and hat that she had purchased for her trip to Scotland. It had been fun showing her sister her new first-class wardrobe she had tailored for her trip.

Jessie's brother-in-law was remarking on the coal strike in the British Isles that was felt worldwide at the time, as they walked past a newsstand showing it mentioned on the front cover of a newspaper.

She heard the young newspaper crier who was selling papers cry out that ship travel schedules in and out of the country were being canceled. Jessie exchanged a look with Maggie and Alex, and mentally noted to check on her return ship itinerary after the business of the day was completed.

The next day, Jessie was escorted by Alex to the White Star Line office in town to inquire about her ticket and travel date, after hearing about the strike. Due to her being a woman, the clerk addressed him instead of her. She stepped up, and standing at her full, slight height, asked him about her first-class ticket booked for the April sailing on the *Oceanic.*

Jessie was told that the White Star Line had a dilemma, given the coal strike, with the much-anticipated maiden voyage of their ship the *Titanic* scheduled to set sail in early April, just a couple of weeks away. The company canceled all other sailings to reroute any coal they had to the Titanic's maiden voyage due to all of the bookings by celebrities and the very wealthy, as it had been promoted heavily. Over the past year, there were posters, coins, and many promotions in several countries around the world selling passage on the unsinkable Titanic's maiden voyage.

The ship Jessie was to sail home on, the *Oceanic*, was one of many canceled sailings for April, postponing it to an early May departure. All available coal was being redirected to the maiden voyage of the *Titanic* departing on April 10, 1912. Jessie had been booked to return home to the States on the *Oceanic* traveling first-class, the same as her arrival, but since the *Titanic* was the only sailing now scheduled in April, all White Star Line passengers on other ships were being offered passage on the *Titanic* sailing to the States.

The White Star Line's offer to all first-class passengers on their other ships was the option to travel in second-class on *Titanic's* maiden voyage, at an additional cost of $7 to exchange their ticket. This was the only way for Jessie to get home in April but would cost her additional money and take away the rare opportunity to travel in first class.

She had heard that second-class on the *Titanic* was opulent as well but after seeing second-class on the *Oceanic* she couldn't imagine it any differently, and traveling second-class home after using the Railroad pension payout for a first-class trip didn't appeal to her.

The *Titanic* was nearly sold out due to the past year's marketing campaign promoting the sailing in countless countries, with some of the richest people and most well-known celebrities in the world having booked passage aboard the ship.

This was not of interest to Jessie, and she disappointedly would wait to travel home in May. The two of them returned to the house where Maggie and her family were staying without trading in her ticket.

+ + +

The days with Maggie and her family were spent much as they had and she enjoyed her visit, yet as the days went by, Jessie grew more and more restless to be back with the rest of her family and eager to begin the next chapter of her life after being away for months.

She reflected on how God had used her time in Scotland to heal her heart, although it would forever be cracked, and even though everything she saw and did she wanted to share with William, she was ready to try to move on. Yet, she knew a piece of him would always remain in her heart, as the love of her life.

As her restlessness grew she talked with Maggie and Alex, and with their support, Alex agreed to take her back to the White Star Line office in the morning to see if she could still secure second-class passage on the Titanic sailing in three days.

The coal strike had ended a few days earlier but there wasn't enough time for the coal to reach the ships in time for April sailings on any other White Star Line ships other than the Titanic.

When she and Alex arrived at the White Star Line office the next morning, she was questioned about her age. Although she traveled unaccompanied to Scotland, a young woman had to be 30 years old to travel unaccompanied, as it was frowned upon at the turn of the century in England. She had no chaperone available to travel to the States with and would have been stuck far from home for an undetermined amount of time.

Instead of stating her actual age of 26, she stood up as tall as her 4'9" frame allowed, and having no escort to travel with, smiled when he reiterated the age requirement that London had, and stated, "Yes, I will be traveling alone".

After a moment's pause as the ticket agent looked at her, he then went about changing her ticket, as she slowly let out her breath that she hadn't noticed she was holding.

With the *Titanic* departing in two days, she was able to trade in her first-class *Oceanic* ticket for a second-class *Titanic* ticket, #20929, for a price of $7.00. It listed her as a resident of England, perhaps due to her brother-in-law's residential status.

Jessie felt excitement at the realization that she was going home in two days! She couldn't wait to see her parents and siblings. Being back in Scotland and then seeing her older sister caused her to miss the rest of her family all the more. She needed to get back to the house and start packing quickly. She was sailing on the *Titanic*!

# 6

# A Titanic Journey

## April 10, 1912, Wednesday

The morning of her departure home by way of the *Titanic*, Jessie said goodbye to Maggie, Alex, and young Edward. She held on an extra moment to each as she hugged them, not knowing the next time she would see them. She would miss them terribly and cherished the time they had spent together.

Alex was a seaman, and acting as her escort, was accompanying her on the Boat Train from London to the Southampton docks, to assure her safe boarding. It was a pleasant ride on the train, the two of them reminiscing about the past weeks, the children's antics, and speculating about the opulent ship on which she would travel. The *Titanic* was said to be the unsinkable, largest, most luxurious ship afloat. They took turns guessing which celebrities or tycoons she might catch a glimpse of onboard.

As the port came into sight, Alex teased her, "Watch out for the sharks!", as they neared the port stop.

She laughed and brushed him off as they gathered the remains of the apples and cheese Maggie had packed them and grabbed the rest of the items they had brought to their seats. Then they departed the train to hail a carriage to take them, and her luggage, the last mile to the port.

White Star Line, R.M.S. Titanic
*Photo credit: Francis Godolphin Osbourne Stuart / Public Use*

As they made their way in the carriage toward the port Jessie felt her breath catch as she glimpsed the ship.

She stared wide-eyed at the sight of the crowds, other horses and buggies, the occasional car for the affluent, newspaper journalists, photographers, street vendors, and the crush of people all trying to get a glimpse of the *Titanic*. Alex squeezed her hand in reassurance as the carriage came to a stop, met her intelligent, blue, wide eyes, and waited for her slight nod before reaching to depart the carriage and enter the throng around them.

Her brother-in-law, came around to her carriage door and made sure to keep one hand on hers, tucked into his elbow at all times, in the bumping, pushing crowd. Her luggage would be unloaded by the driver for her, and taken to the second-class luggage porter, and she was grateful to not have to navigate that in the crowd too.

The smell of bodies in various states of cleanliness, the horses passing by, the waft of droppings in the street as she stepped around them in tow, and the scent of the ocean, all mingled with the chaos of the roar around her. They passed lines of vendors selling food and memorabilia, and criers selling newspapers, as they made their way toward the ship.

The ship looked massive as they approached, larger than anything she had ever seen. The *Oceanic* had looked quite large to her at the time, and this one was much bigger! It had four enormous stacks in the same yellow-orange color she had seen on the *Oceanic*.

It was different this time, not boarding as a first-class passenger as she had the last time she boarded a ship headed to Scotland on the *Oceanic*. She passed the boarding line that checked all third-class passengers over for lice before they could progress, as she and her brother-in-law made their way down the dock to her line, and she marveled at the difference in the boarding process between the classes. It didn't seem like the same ship that all three classes were boarding, and certainly not the same boarding experience.

Soon, she was in line for boarding with the second-class passengers and had said goodbye to the last familiar face and family member she would see for a while. Alex had made sure she was safely in the boarding process before taking his leave, and in all the chaos surrounding the *Titanic's* maiden voyage and the celebrity passengers, she was grateful for his escort.

It was amazing to think that she had heard there were millionaires, famous athletes, actors, titled aristocrats, and immigrants all to be on board with her. It truly felt like a ship for every walk of life to celebrate today.

The excitement and noise level on the pier was deafening as she made her way through the last few steps onto the ship. She had never seen or heard anything like it! She looked up just as she was about to step onto the ship and it looked huge to her from that angle.

Stepping onto the ship was immediate peace from the outside roar, with beautiful surroundings, although she still felt the excitement in the air for the maiden voyage to depart on the unsinkable *Titanic*. While the outside of the ship was impressive as the largest built, the interior was a level above the *Oceanic* and the beauty felt like a very affluent home or luxurious hall! The woodwork, linoleum flooring, mahogany furniture, handrails, paneling and lighting were all unmatched with beauty and she tried to take it all in as she maneuvered through the other passengers in the corridors.

Jessie found her cabin in second class and, to her surprise, it was as beautiful and roomy as first class had been on the *Oceanic*! She had a sofa, bed, and washbasin, and the room was framed in white painted oak paneling, with mahogany furnishing. She was delighted with that realization and was relieved to have traded in her ticket to come home this month on this amazing ship and a once-in-a-lifetime experience instead of next month on the *Oceanic*.

Second class cabin on the Titanic
*Wikipedia - Public Use*

She had so missed her large family of familiar faces and spaces. Yet, it was incredible to find herself on the *Titanic*, with all that she had heard about it in the newspapers, and how quickly it had come about for her to be there in that moment.

Locating the bathroom down the hall, Jessie thought that it was very tastefully decorated as well, *even though it was a bathroom after all*, she smiled to herself.

She found the impressive and luxurious library, where she grabbed a quick tea and cake for the midday meal. The woodwork shone with a brilliant sheen and the crimson seat cushions seemed fit for royalty.

With a quick stop back at her room to grab her coat and hat against the chill wind, she went up on deck to a crowd of contagious excitement for the departure. It seemed like a dream as she watched the celebration below onshore and heard the roar of the crowd as they waved frantically at the ship prepared to set sail.

Jessie scanned the crowd as she stood on the second-class veranda and felt some warmth in knowing that her brother-in-law was in the sea of faces somewhere, so she joined in waving to the crowd with fervor. She had never seen or imagined such a crowd anywhere before. The excitement was pulsing in the air. The roar was unmatched as the ship prepared to depart.

The crowd remained longer than expected, as did the departure by an hour. This was due to a smaller ship in port almost colliding with the *Titanic* from the undertow caused by the massive propeller but was averted by a mere few feet. At 1:00 pm the *Titanic* finally embarked on its much anticipated maiden voyage.

As Jessie watched the pier become smaller and smaller in the distance, she remained at the deck rail surrounded by cool wind and the smell of salt and sea. As the crowd trickled away to a normal amount of people, and a nominal amount of chatter expected on a given day on deck, Jessie decided to walk around for a while to familiarize herself with the ship layout.

The promenade was beautiful and a comfortable place for people to gather and be above deck. Her face was chilly after being on deck for the past hour but she was still cozy and warm inside her coat and hat.

She marveled as she passed different amenities on the ship, as it had a beautiful library, promenade, and smoking room for second class.

She had heard passengers talk as she passed by, about first-class amenities of a massage room, exercise room, Turkish bath, and even a tennis court! She considered herself well-traveled in her 26 years and had never seen anything like it. Everywhere she looked she was amazed at the detail and beauty in the smaller things on the ship, like the wooden floor slats in places, the ornate handrail, or the light fixtures gleaming their greeting.

Jessie wandered and explored a little longer on deck, with a few smiles and greetings to other ladies on the promenade. The chill was finally starting to seep in, so she headed back to her room and turned her attention to unpacking and deciding what to wear to dress for dinner.

+ + +

After unpacking Jessie walked around the inside of the ship for a bit to familiarize herself with where things were located, marveling again at the luxury of the ship, and then headed back to her cabin. She chatted with a couple of ladies about the weather and the amazing ship and then entered her cabin to rest before finding all of the items she needed to dress for dinner. Dinner was expected to be quite a production if the ship's opulence was any indication.

A little while later, Jessie headed out the door and met one of the ladies in the hall and they headed to locate the dining room.

As she passed a window on her way to dinner, she noticed a ferry of passengers coming to join them onboard from Cherbourg, France where they stopped briefly to pick up more passengers.

She could smell amazing scents as she came nearer the dining room and her stomach reacted with hunger. As she approached the second-class dining hall, the oak wood wall panels and trim, and mahogany chairs caught her eye with its high sheen of polish.

On her way to the second-class dining room, she had noticed first-class passengers down the hall heading to their dining room. She saw luxurious dresses, and bow-tied gentlemen, and heard the waft of the beautiful music of strings.

Second class dining room on the Titanic
*Titanic Wiki / Public Use*

As she entered the dining room for second class, with seating of polished mahogany and crimson trim, and piano music playing, it truly felt like a grand hotel or restaurant in a large city, unparalleled in opulence, lights, wood detail, and décor from any ship she had seen or heard about.

A few steps ahead of her, as she walked towards the tables, there was a young girl of about twelve looking very unsure of the experience. Seeing her and being comfortable with children, Jessie stepped up and offered some words of encouragement to her, giving a smile to the woman beside her, as they walked to a table to take their seats.

They sat at the same table and chatted. The young girl's name was Bertha and she was traveling with her mother, Mrs. Bessie Watt, and they were also from Scotland, traveling to meet Mrs. Watt's husband in Portland, Oregon. Jessie spoke to them for most of the meal and enjoyed the conversation. Hearing the native brogue was a comfort to all three of them with the unfamiliar happenings around them.

One of the passengers sitting at the table near Jessie had seen the Astors headed to dinner, receiving greetings from passengers in the first-class section, almost as if they were hosts in their home. Having traveled first-class herself, she was comfortable there, as well as in second-class, but it was fascinating watching and hearing about the social performances of the aristocrats.

The meal was an art in itself, rivaling the first-class meals on the other ship she had sailed on. There were multiple courses with a variety of meats, sauces, sides, and desserts to follow.

After dinner, she and her new companions took a moment to grab their coats from their cabins and went for a stroll on the open promenade for a breath of fresh air before retiring for the evening after a long eventful day. As they strolled, the three of them met Miss Marion Wright and heard that she was on her way to Portland, Oregon to be married.

This stung like a blow in Jessie's stomach as she thought of her wedding a short year ago, and William. So much had changed. She longed to share the details of her trip to Scotland, the visit to her sister and family, and this unprecedented day on this ship, with William. She silently touched the bracelet and the backcomb she kept close, currently holding up her hair, that William had given her as a wedding gift. Not wanting to bring down the mood of her companions, she forced a smile and joined in the conversation of Miss Wright's upcoming wedding details and let the excitement of the bride calm Jessie as she sent up a prayer and hope for her, for a happy ending.

+ + +

The next day Jessie woke early, after retiring sooner than usual from the eventful day and fresh sea air, and felt rested as she dressed and headed to breakfast. She was eager to find her new companions and not miss a moment of this incredible ship and journey. She found Miss Wright at breakfast but did not see Bertha and her mother, and the two enjoyed an easy conversation.

A little while later, while the ship docked at a new port, Queenstown, Ireland, to pick up more passengers, Jessie was outside reading in a lounge chair on deck, to get some air and enjoy those who chose the promenade.

As she sat her book down for a moment's break, she noticed a gentleman with two young children playing on the deck with a toy and she smiled at how attentive and devoted he was to his young sons, a toddler and another perhaps three years old. Jessie breathed in the fresh sea air and smiled at the little ones as she watched some-one greet the gentleman as Hoffman.

Just then, Mrs. Watt and Bertha joined her to chat, claiming her attention. A few moments later, Jessie waved to Mrs. Kate Buss, whom she had met in the hallway near the cabin and again in the bathroom lounge, as she came over to greet the group of women.

Soon, they headed to their cabins to shed their coats and get ready for lunch. Lunch in the second-class dining room was light and delicious, with enough food to make a dinner out of it if one desired, given so many choices.

**Titanic menus by class**
*RMSTitanicOff/Twitter*

Jessie lingered with tea after the meal, chatting with a couple of her female companions who had come for the meal after the promenade. While enjoying her tea and conversation with her companions, two women joined them. Miss Ellen Toomey and her sister were headed to Indiana and had just boarded at the Queenstown port, and were currently enjoying their first meal on board. Jessie and her companions enjoyed filling the two in on all of the amazing amenities that the ship had to offer.

Jessie glanced out the window as she felt the ship hum back to life after the brief stop.

After an extended visit following the meal, Jessie retired to rest in her cabin, tired from the fresh air and activity of the day. She wanted to be rested for the evening dinner and socializing. When she got up, she felt much more energized and dressed for dinner, excited to get out of the cabin and back into the flow of ship life.

Dinner was another display of food that looked like artwork to Jessie. She and her tablemates enjoyed the social scenes unfolding before them while they savored the many rich dinner choices, and listened to the soft notes of the piano playing. There were choices for all palette types at the meals, from lamb, turkey, seafood, soups, sides, and delectable dessert choices. She truly enjoyed talking with Miss Ellen Toomey and her sister during the meal again. They shared in an Irish lilt, that they were headed to visit relatives in the States. They had her chuckling in her napkin with their wit and whimsical comments.

After dinner, Jessie decided to spend time that evening in the second-class library so she could further chat and play a few games with the other ladies she had met earlier in her journey.

+ + +

The next two days the ship sailed through calm seas and chilly breezes. Jessie was so pleased to have met many new lady companions on this sailing to find for meals or company on deck.

While she enjoyed a lunch of corned beef, roast mutton *(that was exquisite - she had to remember to tell her mother about)*, and dessert, which she had a difficult time choosing between tapioca pudding or apple tart, she observed the gentleman, Hoffman, helping his very young sons at the far end of the dining room. He was very devoted to the young children and Jessie had noticed there was no mother with them. It made her long for home and her siblings all the more.

She was having a peaceful, healing, enjoyable time on a beautiful ship, with delicious food and enjoyable companions. Jessie was beginning to feel a little bit like herself after the roller coaster and tragedy of the year past.

Since her husband's death, life had not been what it was before for her. Seeing her homeland and grandparents, her sister and family, and meeting new friends, she reflected on the fact that she was longing to return to her family and her unknown future. Or, at least, she was ready to think about an unknown future. That was an improvement over the last six months.

Her smooth, enjoyable sailing was nearing its end in a couple days, as was her journey, and Jessie had a train ticket already purchased to get home from the port. She was about to begin her next chapter in life, and she had hope again for the future. That felt good to Jessie, feeling some light from the long darkness after losing William.

# 7

## A Titanic Tragedy

*April 14, 1912, Sunday*

The following morning, Jessie awoke energized and ready for the day. She looked out the porthole window at the ocean as she went about her morning meal and routine, marveling at the calm seas, even though she had heard the water temperature was no more than 28 degrees. She wondered how marine life could survive those temperatures this far out to sea in such cold, and she thought for the hundredth time how glad she was that the ship was said to be unsinkable.

She smiled to herself remembering her brother-in-law's comment, "Watch out for sharks!", while they rode the boat train to the port, as they both knew the ship wouldn't sink based on all the information they had heard about the newly designed ship. Jessie had heard talk of the 16 watertight compartments that the ship had and if any of them were breached, the others kept the boat afloat. Although she had never really worried much about that on her ship travels in the past, it was comforting to know since this was such a big ship with over 2000 people aboard.

In three days, she would be back in the States, and she felt comfort that her train ticket back home was tucked away in her purse. There hadn't been time to write to her family before departure, having decided two days before sailing to journey on the *Titanic* instead of the *Oceanic* so she wouldn't have to wait the extra month to come home. She would beat any letter that would have been sent home to alert them of the ship change anyway. Jessie was eager to surprise her family and tell them all about this opulent ship that she had been able to sail on after all of the promotions everyone had seen or heard about the *Titanic* leading up to its maiden voyage. She felt very thankful for the experience and God's provision.

It had been a good day chatting with her lady friends and playing a few games in the library to pass the time.

Dinner was amazing again, with several delectable choices, and she favored the roasted turkey and cranberry sauce, rounding it out with plum pudding - what her family called Christmas pudding at home. This was a traditional dinner during the holiday for her family, and it brought her comfort as she drew nearer to her home and the people she loved.

She briefly chatted with a table mate, Lawrence Beesley, a widower with an eleven-year-old son at home or school. Lawrence had recently resigned from a university and was headed to visit the States, then on to see his brother in Toronto.

After dinner, she attended a church service held that evening in the dining room of the second cabin where Reverend Mr. Carter, of the Whitechapel district in London, led them all in prayer for the safe arrival of the ship. The reverend was on his way to visit a brother in Kansas City, so they all benefited from having him onboard to lead the service.

Jessie had been busy all day enjoying her time onboard, so she decided to retire to her cabin after dinner and seek some rest for the day ahead.

+ + +

Jessie changed into her night clothes and decided to read for a while. Her mind stirred with the reflection of the day's experiences, so a short time later, she decided to write some letters to capture her experiences while they were fresh in her mind. She wouldn't finish the letters yet but add to them during her journey. Jessie finished her updates to the letters and promptly fell asleep.

She was suddenly shaken awake and tried to clear the fog in her mind from sleep to understand what had woke her so abruptly. She glanced at the mantle clock which showed 11:45 pm, and sleepily looked around the room.

She knew something had shaken her, so she looked out the window and saw what looked like a mountain of ice very near the ship passing by, with a top that looked like a double tooth root that's been pulled, appearing very jagged on top.

Jessie jumped out of bed and rushed up to the next deck.

There, the steward told her and the other women who had rushed up near her, "Nothing bad has happened. Get back to your quarters and be quiet".

His mannerisms and tone, talking to ladies that way, did not match what his words were saying, but they obeyed the order and headed back to their cabins.

Once back in her cabin, Jessie listened but didn't hear any chaos or anyone sounding an alarm, as she remained awake listening for a few minutes. She noticed the boat felt silent now, with no humming or vibration as it had been when she fell asleep to the light, rhythmic sound of the engines. She felt uneasy due to the proximity of the iceberg she had seen out her window, the shaking she had felt, the quiet of the engines, and the steward's clipped response. But, decided she must be alright based on his statements.

Jessie tried to relax on her bed since no crew member came to alert them, and she began to get sleepy again. Yet, she did notice that the ship was not fully level anymore with a slight shift but assumed things were under control, whatever it was. Maybe it was just one of the 16 watertight compartments that was damaged from the iceberg which accounted for the slight list.

## April 15, 1912

Before Jessie could fully fall asleep again, at 12:30 am a hard knock made her jump, followed by the purser of the second cabin ordering those in her hallway to get up, put on life preservers, and get on deck.

His demeanor and tone had the ladies all in a state of fear and urgency now and they quickly followed his commands. Jessie grabbed her warm coat to put over her nightclothes, and her hat and boots this time, thinking she would be standing in the cold for a while before hearing the all-clear of danger passed. Then she fit her life preserver over her coat.

Out in the hall, she recognized Dr. Alfred Pain, a young twenty-four-year-old doctor, and he led the group of women that had gathered in the corridor up to the deck. When she arrived on deck with the other second-class passengers whose cabins were near hers, it took a few moments for her head to comprehend what her eyes were seeing.

She stood wide-eyed, with her feet frozen at the deck landing from where she had just come as other passengers either shoved around her or were also slowed to a halt trying to take in the chaos that ensued. She found the men making lifeboats ready, with crowds pushing to get on.

She saw women passengers quickly being herded into the nearby lifeboat, with their men close behind. Some women were fighting not to leave their husbands as their spouses tried to encourage them to get on a lifeboat, some bodily being put in the boats. Men with raised voices trying to secure a seat in a lifeboat, and people running and pushing to an urgent destination.

Jessie could feel the ship list strongly now and see people trying to keep their balance in a state of flurry. Immediately realizing that the ship may be lost and before she could even think it through, she ran back to her berth to grab her wedding gifts from William, the bracelet and backcomb for her hair. She also grabbed her purse containing her train ticket home and her checkbook, then headed back up to the boat deck.

Jessie's purse

Having no organized directions, Jessie did not know where she was supposed to go. Being of small stature, she felt contact on her shoulders and back as she was pushed about by passengers running to and fro, all trying to figure out how to get to safety. While she looked around for a lifeboat, Jessie recognized John Jacob Astor, the real estate tycoon, and multimillionaire American social elite, as he

Jessie's purse
inside

tried in vain to get in a lifeboat, but only women and children were being allowed. When he failed to get on a lifeboat, to her horror, she saw him jump overboard after a lifeboat was lowered without him.

She lost track of time, and her mind filtered seemingly useless bits of information, such as the music of the string group on board playing, men saying goodbye to crying women, the smell of something burning, smoke and flashes of light from flares, the freezing water temperature, black water, the stillness of the night, which made the air all the more crisp - as she tried to figure out where to go. Time seemed to stand still.

Suddenly a seaman grabbed her amid the chaos and roughly placed her in Lifeboat #9. Perhaps due to her size and the emergent situation, he thought she was an older child based on how he grabbed her and placed her. She looked around wide-eyed after being placed roughly into the boat. She saw the faces of shock and terror around her.

As a pretty French girl stumbled getting into the lifeboat, Jessie glanced around with heavy relief to see twelve-year-old Miss Bertha Watts, Miss Kate Buss, Miss Ellen Toomey, and Miss Marion Wright in her boat. She could only hope the others that she had met on the ship were already afloat in another lifeboat.

While the lifeboat was being prepared to lower into the sea, Jessie looked around for anything to cling to in the boat, to keep from falling out into the freezing water, as it swayed back and forth.

Then, someone quickly placed a toddler into her lap and she instantly recognized him as the youngest of the two Hoffman boys she had seen on deck and while dining. She frantically scanned the boat occupants to hand him to his father, and upon not seeing him, she quickly scanned the fearful faces along the side of the boat, mostly men watching their women disappear on boats into the dark night but saw no face of his father. Jessie inquired of his brother and father to anyone within hearing distance and was told by a nearby passenger that the other little one was put in another boat, and no one had seen the father since then.

Chaos was happening all around her with people frantic to get to safety.

As the lifeboat lowered past the deck levels, two young men jumped from the ship, one after the other, with a hard landing, hitting some of the passengers as they made it into the boat. She recognized one of the jumpers as a young pastor she had seen on the ship earlier, who carried a walking stick, and he was still clinging to the stick after he landed in the boat.

She grabbed the toddler close and hung on tight to him with one hand, and to the cross board that was her seat with the other, and continued to hold on throughout the uneven lowering. There was sudden panic to get the ropes untied as the boat veered to one end, followed by the jarring splash of the lifeboat as it was released into the sea, listing heavily, and coming to settle afloat.

One of the seamen pointed to a gentleman in the water and said it was John Jacob Astor. Jessie shielded the toddler's face as they passed many people in the water while rowing away from the ship. There were shouts, screams, and splashing all around their boat and some people appeared to be asleep floating in their life jackets. Her heart ached for every one of them as she looked around stunned, and all she could do was hold on to the toddler, realizing that was the extent of whom she could help.

She exchanged wide-eyed looks with her friends seated around the boat, and there were no words for any of them, just silent tears. There were about 40 women and children, the two young men who jumped in, and six seamen on the boat.

Jessie watched in horror as their boat rowed away from the *Titanic*, knowing that all of the people she could hear and see still on the ship did not have a way to safety. Every bump on the boat as they rowed away from the ship made Jessie want to put her hands over her ears, not knowing if it was debris or bodies, and she covered the toddler's ears in her arms.

As they rowed farther, the people she saw in the water, who must have been submerged longer, had a range of frozen expressions on their faces against the black of the water. It was unthinkable, all of it, and the sights were more than her mind could absorb all at once.

The boat occupants watched the huge ship as they rowed slowly away. The *Titanic* was listing heavily now as it continued its slow descent into the deep.

*What about all of the people still onboard*, her mind screamed.

Titanic Lifeboat of Passengers
*Wikimedia Commons / Public Use*

It occurred to her that she didn't see any third-class passengers in the lifeboats, either hers, or in the other lifeboats she had seen loading, or in the couple that she could make out in the darkness of the open, black sea. All of the fathers, brothers, sons, and many other women and children that she had seen from third class would be lost, as her lifeboat drifted slowly away to the rhythm of the oars being pulled by the seamen. She hoped they were on other lifeboats that she didn't see.

Jessie had seen men of all classes in the water at various stages of splashing, swimming, and sleeping. She was thinking she would gladly have given up her seat to keep a family together when her attention was caught by the toddler crying in her lap.

She hugged the child close, saying, "Shhh, it will be alright. I'm with you. I'll keep you warm, wee cherub. Here, let me wrap you in my coat."

She was better able to shield the child from what was unfolding before them, while keeping him warm, wrapped in her coat with her. She was thankful for it, as many in her boat were in night clothes and slippers with no shield from the cold.

The *Titanic* was going down fast, as the screams of those in the water, those falling overboard, or those still on the ship reached her lifeboat. The passengers in her lifeboat could do nothing but pray, cry, and watch. It was more than one could bear.

# 8

## Black Water and Ice

Jessie's lifeboat was about half a mile away when the *Titanic* last saw the night sky and sank. The ship lights were still on until the last moments when the ship seemed to tilt up and sink into the depths of the sea.

Then the silence came. And the bitter cold. The lifeboat was surrounded by black water.

Many of the lifeboat passengers were suffering from the cold in their night clothes and slippers, yet some had grabbed their coats like Jessie did. The seamen had wool uniforms and took turns paddling the oars which helped to warm them.

Jessie observed that the women, though lightly dressed, seemed to stand the cold better than the men. She also reflected that the women seemed more composed than the men on the *Titanic* during the chaos of the tragedy too. This was the opposite of what she would have thought.

In her lifeboat, those looking after children needed to be strong for them, while the others focused more on their discomfort.

In the hours that followed floating in the ocean, there was much time to think. Jessie felt that someone with a family should be in her seat instead of her. Feeling ungrateful from that thought, she raised her head, taking a break from constant prayer and from snuggling the toddler's head to save as much warmth between them as she could, and looked up. Looking for stars in the black void, she thanked God for His provision in rescuing her from the ship, as well as those also in the lifeboats. She needed to stay positive to get through this moment, as her heart ached for families torn apart.

Then, as thought fragments floated in her mind, she recalled a moment when she heard Mr. Hoffman call the toddler, Edmond, on deck. And she added thanks to God for having her care for little Edmond, as by being a comfort to him, like she had done for young ones most of her years growing up with a family of eleven kids, was also a comfort to her.

Although there was little to no talk in her boat, Jessie was grateful to have her friend's presence as a comfort in her lifeboat with her as well.

It was terribly cold, uncomfortably still, and fearfully black. The sea was so calm she could only hear the lap of the occasional oars now, in the black water, as well as people occasionally repositioning seeking any warmth. One couldn't see where the water ended and the night sky and stars began.

She was grateful for no waves as she didn't know how the lifeboat passengers could have survived the icy cold splashes of waves in the freezing temperature. Jessie could barely feel her fingers and took extra care to ensure that little Edmond's hands and feet were snuggly tucked in the warmth that was left between them. He had fallen asleep in the aftermath of the tragedy, and she was glad he did.

There was a lot of time, hours, to just think in the silence, and try to process what had happened. Yet, as with any trauma, thoughts came in snippets and flashes. The memory of her brother-in-law's jest about sharks came to mind for Jessie, and how bad he would feel when the news reached them that her ship sank. She would have laughed if it were another time.

+ + +

The hours of extreme cold and rhythmic movement of the lifeboat were hypnotic and the passengers were silent from the trauma, yet they kept nudging one another not to fall asleep in the cold. Fighting to stay warm enough, being awake a day and a night, and the tragedy drained everyone, and sleep was tugging strongly at them. There were times that Jessie fought back sleep hard, as she had to keep the little one in her lap safe and warm as best she could.

After a while, most of the passengers had gone silent in voice and tears, while attention turned to surviving the cold, then someone let out a shout that broke the long silence. Some lights were spotted on the horizon by the lifeboats, hers and those around them, and they thought it could be flares of a ship.

One of the seamen in her lifeboat, deckhand Patty McGough, suddenly thundered, "Let us all pray to God, for there is a ship on the horizon and it's making for us!"

After the eerie silence of the past hours, this broke the night like a thunderclap and gave them some hope, although there was no way to gauge how far away the ship lights were, how long it would take to reach them, or if they even knew the lifeboats were there afloat.

The lights in the distance became a mainstay throughout the night hours, and in the black sky of night the lights grew brighter and the lifeboat passengers could see that the lights were indeed a ship slowly getting closer.

Soon, they could see a ship headed for them. As it grew in view, it grew in size and was headed right for the lifeboats. Thank God!

With the ship lights coming closer, Jessie and her fellow passengers could now make out other lifeboats all around them in the distance that had drifted away from each other. Yet, they were all now rowing to get closer to the ship's path. Soon, in the distance, Jessie could see the lifeboats nearest the ship drawing next to it to unload the passengers. One by one, lifeboats ahead of them unloaded their passengers, but it took time as the lifeboats were scattered in the area.

For what seemed like days, was almost four more hours, until it was Lifeboat #9's turn to be unloaded onto the ship in the predawn hours. The lifeboat pulled alongside the ship, which Jessie could now see was called the *Carpathia*, and passengers unloaded one at a time, very carefully up a ladder, given the now rolling waves of the ship hitting the lifeboat. Frozen feet, slippers, evening shoes, various stages of dress, and frozen fingers made it a slow process to unload each passenger from the bobbing lifeboat and up the ladder to the deck of the Carpathia.

Once Edmond was safely onboard, he was ushered away, presumably to find his family members, but Jessie felt the loss from her arms after so long caring for him. She lost sight of him on the ship and hoped he would find his father and brother.

There was a seaman from the *Carpathia* asking for names as passengers came aboard. He had to write down names the best he could, quickly, translating all of the accents of the passengers, with the tendency of dialects increasing under stress.

When it was her turn, she gave her name, "Jessie Trout", and followed the other passengers to find warmth and get out of the sea.

The *Carpathia* had been bound out of New York to the Mediterranean, heard the distress call of the *Titanic*, and had traveled fifty-eight miles in three and a half hours in response to the *Titanic's* call.

Other ships had been closer but knowing the presumably unsinkable structure of the ship and that it was the maiden voyage they didn't believe the calls of distress. One ship close by at the time of the disaster had mistakenly thought the flares were celebrations for the maiden voyage, and continued away on it's route. The *Titanic* disaster was the first use of the newly adopted international Morse Code reserved to signal for help, so this reached several ships.

Once aboard, passengers on the *Carpathia* helped *Titanic* survivors with spare coats, clothes, shoes, and some cabins. The survivors were served brandy and hot coffee to warm them, and they were given places on the boat to rest, with some of the passengers turning their stateroom over to the new guests. Many who grieved throughout the night from leaving behind loved ones to board a lifeboat were experiencing overwhelming grief anew as lifeboat after lifeboat was rescued and no sign of their husband, son, or loved one was found.

Jessie hadn't realized how hungry she had been until the hot soup was given to her with some bread. She ate it quicker than manners dictated, as she looked around for the first time, at the faces of survivors. They looked as blank as she felt, from the shock and tragedy.

The first lifeboat was rescued by the *Carpathia* at 4:10 am and the last lifeboat at 8:50 am. Of the 2229 people aboard the *Titanic*, 705 survivors were rescued by the *Carpathia*. Lifeboat #9 was rescued at 7:00 am.

Of the 93 women in second class on the *Titanic*, all made it with the exception of fifteen souls.

Titanic survivors on the Carpathia
*Wikipedia / Public Use*

Jessie, along with most of the survivors, was quiet and subdued. The survivors sat in groups, huddled together sipping warm drinks, trying to stay out of the chilly breeze as the *Carpathia* sailed back to New York, where it had recently departed on a transatlantic route.

The *Titanic* passengers seemed to want to be near one another, as companions that needed little words, so talk stayed at the level that courtesy demanded. No one was ready to talk of their lost loved ones, or what they had seen, heard, and experienced, they only longed to feel warm with dry land under their feet.

There were so many sad stories of lost family members, but the reunited ones always brought tears to Jessie's eyes to watch. One story was about a husband, wife, and baby, all thinking the other was lost, having been on all different lifeboats, and finding each other once onboard the *Carpathia*.

Jessie Trout, Hilda Slayter, Lawrence
Beesley on the R.M.S. Carpathia
*Encyclopedia Titanica / Public Use*

Miraculously, Jessie found all of her new lady friends had survived! They huddled together on the deck, having silently all decided they didn't want to be below deck after the sinking, except when absolutely necessary.

Jessie was in a conversation with Miss Fannie Kelly, who was in Lifeboat #9 with Jessie, and other survivors on the deck of the Carpathia, all from second class.

She wandered down the deck to a couple other familiar faces from the *Titanic* and joined in their conversation. Someone onboard the *Carpathia* had a camera and asked the three of them to pose for a photograph. Jessie stood alongside second-class passengers Lawrence Beesley, wearing a bathrobe borrowed from a first-class passenger on the Carpathia, and Miss Hilda Slayter, traveling single and rerouted to the *Titanic* from another sailing, the same as Jessie.

She had a brief thought that she was wearing the same coat and hat as the day she took the family photograph with her sister's family and the picture she used as her passport photo. At that moment, the memory seemed like a different lifetime to Jessie.

The three nights on the Carpathia passed in a blur, and it seemed it was spent nibbling food and seeking warmth, as that was all she could bring herself to do.

The survivors of the *Titanic* would arrive on the *Carpathia* in New York City that night.

# 9

## To Their Surprise

*April 18, 1912, Thursday*

The *Carpathia* docked in New York City shortly after 9:00 p.m. It seemed appropriate to be raining since that mirrored the mood of the *Titanic* survivors as the ship docked.

Even at that late hour, and in rainy conditions, the docks were overflowing with people, newspaper journalists, photographers, family and friends of passengers, and onlookers. Once in port, on the way to dock, reporters and journalists were on tug boats alongside the *Carpathia* yelling questions with megaphones to survivors about the sinking. Most survivors stayed quiet, averting their eyes, as their focus was on getting back on dry, solid footing.

Jessie nervously glanced at the black water slapping along the ship and dock as she debarked from the ship onto land. She had never felt so relieved to be walking on land in her life!

It was all overwhelming for Jessie, and there was no one to greet her, having not been able to tell her family in time before sailing. Reporters, photographers and well wishers were in the faces of the survivors as they disembarked, while they sought transportation and love ones.

About one hundred passengers who did not have family meeting them or anywhere to go for the night were immediately taken to St. Vincent's Hospital. It was late that night when they arrived and they were given food, clothing, and medical attention.

Jessie was very grateful to get a dress and a pair of shoes and to get out of her night clothes after days of wearing them.

It was discovered at the hospital that several of the survivors had frozen feet and needed assistance, yet Jessie had managed to stave off freezing with her winter outerwear over her nightclothes. Some of the women only had nightclothes and thin night shoes on, with which to combat the long hours in the cold while they were on the lifeboats and *Carpathia*.

Having arrived at the hospital late, and changing clothes, the survivors were provided a light meal and a bed, which Jessie fell onto fully dressed with exhaustion. *It was the first time she felt warm in days*, she thought, and promptly fell asleep.

The next day the passengers were given a purse of $25 each, that had been collected from the citizens of New York, and they rested and ate filling meals, while volunteers helped them all find and organize transportation to their homes.

Jessie had her train ticket already in her handbag, so she was assisted with departure times and a ride to the station planned for the the next day. Jessie was very grateful for all the help from the hospital and citizens, as all she had left from her many possessions was her nightclothes, coat, boots, hat, handbag with her checkbook inside, and the beloved bracelet and hair comb. With all of their help and her train ticket home in her handbag, she would head for home in the morning.

+ + +

After a light breakfast provided by the church and a ride to the bus station the next morning, Jessie was seated on the train and still trying to steady her shaking hands that would start shaking randomly, accompanied by a sense to flee. She realized it was a response to the trauma and worked on steadying her breathing to fight it off.

The hours passed quickly as she faded in and out of sleep in her seat, being exhausted from all that she had endured for the past few days. She would fall asleep, to suddenly jerk awake with the train movement and tragic images in her dreams. All she knew was she had food that she had brought on the train and she was warm. That was enough security for now to rest. She napped in short sessions because if she slept too long nightmares and the flashes of the sinking ship experience, that she pushed away when awake, flashed before her closed eyes.

She arrived in Columbus at 1:45 p.m. on Sunday. She couldn't believe it was only one week ago, last Sunday, that the unsinkable, luxurious *Titanic* sank to the bottom of the sea, taking 1,500 passengers with it. She teared up at the thought, as she waited her turn to disembark from the train. It was still incomprehensible.

There was no one to greet her, which was a bit disappointing to her. She knew her family had no prior knowledge that she was traveling on the *Titanic*, or was in the disaster, but she had heard that survivor names were listed in the newspapers around the country, and thought they may have seen her name.

Jessie carefully avoided debarking passengers as they hugged their family or friends and, having only the clothes on her back and a handbag, headed to find a carriage to take her home.

She secured a driver and noticed it was the same carriage driver who dropped her off at the train station with many bags and boxes just a few months ago.

When the carriage driver asked her if she had luggage to load, she answered, "No, just me".

He paused looking at her puzzled, then replied. "Very well, ma'am. Where to?"

She was headed to her sister's home, and told the driver, "Please take me to Mrs. George Findley's, at 184 Princeton Avenue".

She had received a letter while in London from her mother that said her father was relocating from the Johnson Farm, near Camp Chase, to Winnipeg, Manitoba, Canada, and her mother was residing with her sister, Georgina, in Columbus temporarily during the transition.

She arrived at Georgina's home where her mother was staying, and the shock and drain of the tragedy finally seemed to hit her like a brick wall, as she finally felt safe and warm.

Her mother hurriedly entered the front room from the kitchen while drying her hands on a rag asking, "Who is here? Jessie! I didn't expect you as I hadn't received word of your return", as she threw her arms around her daughter.

Jessie was enveloped in her mother's hug, as her sister, with her infant on her hip, and two kids trailing behind, joined them from various reaches of the house. A minute later, her sister's husband, George, who had been in his study, entered to see what the noise was about.

George greeted her and stated he would go unload her luggage, but Jessie held up her hand and stopped him.

"I don't have any luggage with me," she stated. He looked puzzled, having known she planned an extended trip when she departed, and she added, "It's at the bottom of the sea."

Finally, the tears came while safe in her mother's embrace, and in the warmth of her sister's home.

+ + +

After the initial shock of her statement retreated, her mother soothed Jessie and helped her take off her coat, hat, and handbag, and guided her to sit down, then brought some light refreshments.

"Start at the beginning, please", George encouraged.

Jessie had tried to push the images out of her mind the past several days, but they all came flooding back while she told of her long journey with the tragic ending. There were tears in the eyes of the family listening and her sister had them running down her cheeks. Jessie received hugs, touches of concern, and words of reaction as she told the story. It was still too much to comprehend. Perhaps, it would always be.

Her mother knew her daughter's plan to return home in April on the White Star Line ship, the *Oceanic*. Having a mother's concern, and the need to reassure herself of her daughter's safety, she had scoured the newspaper list of *Titanic* survivors and saw that Jessie wasn't listed, so she and the family were relieved.

Jessie found out that the newspaper listed her as *Jessie Tant* when they printed the survivor list, having been a mistake when written down on the *Carpathia,* or when someone read the handwriting on the list. She wondered how many other passengers that may have happened to as well.

When she had finished recounting her story, Georgina urged her upstairs for a hot bath, and to find some dresses that would fit Jessie until she could get some new ones. That sounded amazing to Jessie, and the mere thought of being clean after the past many days would be luxurious, but she was so drained it took her sister taking her arm to guide her upstairs for her to get started.

The story spread quickly, maybe from the explanation she gave the carriage driver, maybe from George sharing with his colleagues, she didn't know, but that evening a *Columbus Citizen* newspaper reporter showed up and asked her, as the first *Titanic* survivor to return to Columbus, if she would tell her story for printing on the front page of the newspaper the next day.

She had eaten lunch, bathed, put on a dress her sister found for her, rested for a little bit, and now safe with her family, she was feeling much more herself. Feeling more mentally clear after talking about it earlier with her family, she figured it may help her process the tragedy if she shared it, and agreed to the interview. She told of all of the details that she could remember, including the names of her ship friends that she had made, seeing Astor die, and caring for Edmond.

Word spread quickly of a local *Titanic* survivor and shortly after, two other newspapers, *The Columbus Dispatch* and *Ohio State Journal* also interviewed her.

+ + +

As the days passed, Jessie felt more at peace during the day and tried to fight off the images of the tragedy by night.

Georgina was happy to have her stay at her home as Jessie tried to find her equilibrium from losing William, and the *Titanic* sinking, to figure out her next direction in life. Jessie enjoyed her days with her sister, helping her around the house, and going on errands with her. She adored spending time with the little ones to help her sister and get to know the young ones better.

Jessie was a very intelligent woman, but women were just starting to work, although she didn't know many that did, and women didn't live alone as she would prefer. She also was not in the mindset to look for a husband and had become accustomed to making her own decisions for herself in the past nine months.

The newspapers continued to report the recovery of bodies from the *Titanic* through April and May, with search ships being sent out to retrieve bodies and either bury them at sea or bring them back for burial in Halifax, depending on the condition of the body. On one ship retrieval route, up to 328 bodies had been recovered from the site, one newspaper reported.

Many stories of the tragedy were coming out and there was an ongoing investigation by the British Board of Trade. It was reported that the *Titanic* received six reports of ice in the water and a seventh report warning of the location of the iceberg, which was supposed to be shouted up to the bridge but never reached the Captain of the *Titanic*. In May, the investigation led to the decision that if the last of the seven ice warnings had reached the captain and been heeded, as it was the only one to mention the location of the iceberg, the disaster could have been avoided. If there had been enough lifeboats for all passengers then many more lives would have been spared. A new law was in the making at that time to ensure that enough lifeboat seats for all passengers would be provided on ships in the future.

Jessie had seen a story in the newspaper about the Hoffman children, seeing them referred to as the "French Orphans" while they searched for a relative to claim the the little boys in New York. Their names turned out to be Michel and Edmond Navratil.

"French Orphans" Michel and Edmond Navratil
*Wikipedia / Public Use*

Edmond's older brother had been put in another lifeboat and the brothers had been reunited. Their father did not survive the sinking.

Their mother had been located and reunited with them a month after the fateful night when Jessie and Edmond had shared each other's warmth for survival. It was reported that the mother had no idea they had been on the Titanic, as the father had whisked them away from their mother in France, planning to make a new start in the States.

Jessie was very happy to hear of the reunion so she could quit wondering about Edmond's welfare.

A few weeks after her return home, Jessie was notified of a lawsuit being filed against the White Star Line and she decided to join the lawsuit to sue the White Star Line shipping company, although she didn't know if anything would come of it. It was the principal.

While she waited for all of the courts, newspaper stories, and discussions of the disaster to die down, she wondered what the next part of her life would bring as she longed for peaceful, safe horizons.

# 10

## Hope and Fireflies

*Early Fall 1912*

Some time passed, and things calmed down as much as could be expected, and once again daily routine returned. Jessie's sister, Georgina, and her mother, along with other family members who spent time at the house, were a great help to Jessie as she healed from her experiences. She loved spending time with her little niece and nephews.

Her nightmares were infrequent now, and whether she didn't want to talk about it, or wanted to share a bit of it, her family was there as support. However, she couldn't seem to shake an extreme reaction at random, minor things, as she would quickly shy away and her heart would race. This was lessening as the months passed, at least the outward signs of it were improving, but the racing heart reacting to certain sudden things wasn't going away.

As routine returned, Jessie turned her thoughts to her path and her future plan. She didn't have a place or role. Her sister was gracious in letting her stay, and she fully enjoyed her time helping her with chores and shopping but she couldn't stay forever. Her parents would welcome her in Canada, but she didn't want to live off of them and wanted a life of her own. She didn't know what to do.

It was in this mindset that she planned to visit her sister, Maggie, in Minnesota since they had returned to the States. It was late summer and a good time for travel to avoid the sudden snowstorms of the winter months. It was time to give her sister, Georgina, and her sister's family time without another live-in guest.

Saying goodbye to Georgina and her mother was harder than she anticipated the morning of departure. Since the *Titanic* disaster, she treasured time with her family all the more, as tomorrow was not guaranteed. The two sisters, their mother, and George gathered arm in arm on the porch of the house to pray for safe travel. Georgina and her husband must have sensed the uneasy feeling Jessie was experiencing, as it was her first trip away from her makeshift home since the ship's sinking, and they lingered longer in their goodbye as a comfort to Jessie. Before long, she was in the carriage headed to the train station.

She boarded the train, settled in, and began to relax to the hum of the train moving along the rails, and thought briefly that she was happy to be traveling on land and not sea this time around. It was also exhilarating to be traveling alone once again.

Jessie had a relaxing, smooth trip to Maggie's home, from the travel and the food she had packed, being greeted by her sister at the station, securing her still sparse luggage, and the expedited carriage ride to the house in White Bear Lake, Minnesota where her sister was living.

+ + +

## Minnesota - Fall 1912

Jessie enjoyed Minnesota and the 'out west' feel of the environment, and the beauty of the lakes and greenery, although she doubted she would feel so inclined towards it in the winter months when her sister could be snowed in for days on end, in White Bear Lake.

After a few weeks of settling in and getting to know the area a bit with Maggie, she was ready to join her on some social outings.

There was a fall picnic planned not far away from the house, in St. Cloud, at a central park, and Maggie and Jessie packed a lunch for the family, some blankets to sit on, and they all headed to St. Cloud.

It was a pleasantly warm fall day and the leaves were beginning to change to shades of yellow and orange, along with a shift in the coolness of the breeze.

Jessie enjoyed the people she met and saw groups of people enjoying themselves. She stood up to go check on the children playing nearby for Maggie and slowly walked past a large oak tree with her eyes fixed on the kids with a smile. Jessie nearly bumped into a gentleman that she had seen earlier talking with a group of men in the distance, and he made an unexpected pleasant comment, as she excused herself. The note of humor in it caught her attention.

He was taller than her by several inches, with light eyes that matched her own, on the thinner side, and while he seemed reserved, he had the eyes and wit of intelligence.

They chatted with easy banter, surrounded by parents and older girls nearby, keeping an eye on the children who were chasing one another and playing games with shrieks of laughter.

His name was Harvey, and he seemed wise on many subjects. He had an interesting job, a herdsman and trail leader, driving Oxen for wagon trains of immigrants settling out west, and the group of men he had been with when she noticed him earlier were of the same type of profession. She learned that St. Cloud was a wagon and oxen rest area for immigrants looking to settle in the Dakotas, which brought him through there often.

Harvey stated that he usually headed out within a day or two, to return to Pennsylvania for a short visit with his family, and then back to Chicago to pick up the herds of the next wagon train. The immigrant families who hired him would sail into New York, then come up the Erie Canal to Chicago where he would meet up with them for the journey out West.

He mentioned to Jessie that he was going to stay around for a bit this time, and seemed to have a smile teasing the corners of his mouth. Jessie had glanced at him as he was speaking, and this caused her to look back, and then down with a slight rise of heat to her face.

Over the weeks to follow, Harvey called on Jessie, at Maggie's home, for short visits or walks, and even joined the family for dinner.

Nellie's Prized Scottish Shortbread

Ingredients:

1 Cup butter

½ Cup sugar

1 egg yoke

2 Cups flour

Preheat the oven to 325 degrees.

Soften the butter slightly, but don't let it become oily. Stir in sugar and egg yoke with a wooden spoon. Turn onto a lightly floured board and knead lightly while adding in the 2 cups of flour until the lump cracks. Divide into two parts. Pat each part into a separate ungreased pie plate (pan). Pierce with a fork. OR, cut into squares and put directly onto a baking sheet. Bake at 325-350 degrees until lightly browned.

The key to this recipe is drawing and kneading the 2 cups of flour into the butter mixture.

Enjoy, and put the teapot on lassie!

**Nellie's Prized Scottish Shortbread Recipe**
*Kelley Senkowski / no use without permission*

One evening with the family, he shared stories over beef stew followed by shortbread (her sister Nellie's recipe that had been passed around the family) and tea. He was also from a large family of ten children and he was second from the youngest in placement.

As the family listened intently to Harvey's stories after dinner, they laughed in surprise as he shared, "I can make dinner for you next time. I practiced on the trail and can hit a jackrabbit with my bullwhip in one hit from a wagon. That knocks it goofy so I can grab it and gut it for dinner."

He was born in Glen Rock, Pennsylvania, to Elizabeth Virgina Gantz Bortner and Michael Kerchner Bortner, and once the sons turned sixteen in his family, the boys were sent out to find their way in the world. He was a day laborer at sixteen, and then a few years later ended up as a herdsman, to be able to travel and see other places. He was an avid reader of the New York Times and whatever local paper was available in the town he was in at the time.

Harvey would entertain Jessie with stories on their walks. He was fascinated with the history of Deadwood, South Dakota, and visited it when he was in that area. He often brought up tidbits of stories from the history of Deadwood to entertain Jessie.

One day, they were walking on an unseasonably warm winter day, down the street from her sister's home. Jessie was glad for the chance to get out of the house after a snowy winter during a warming trend that melted the snow. Trees of birch, elm, and oak, awaiting new leaves were randomly lined along the street, and a welcome sight from the walls of the house. As they strolled, she was grateful that dress styles were now closer fitting, more comfortable, straight skirts, with fabrics not trailing behind or full, and without the cumbersome dress layers of her youth.

They passed a couple of children eager for Spring to arrive, who were taking the warmer day to get outside and sell hot drinks to passersby along the street. They offered some to Jessie and Harvey, in a new type of cup, called a Dixie cup, that could be thrown away after use.

*What a strange concept,* she thought.

They gave the young lady and her brother a penny and enjoyed the warm refreshment next to a large maple tree. Harvey soon had her giggling to his story from the trail of leading cattle for wagons, and all that the experiences and adventures entailed.

Jessie felt at ease with Harvey, he was stable, and intelligent, while also reserved, and he could carry on thoughtful conversation. He was well-read about the happenings in the world, so they were able to have discussions on current and past events.

Harvey liked Jessie's ability to have intelligent conversations too, not being afraid to have her own opinions, but that she was also a gentle person, and wonderful with her sister's children.

Soon, the two of them were talking of love and a future together. During the holidays and before Jessie knew it, they were planning a wedding while she was still in Minnesota! They would all venture up to Winnipeg, Canada, were her parents and some siblings were living and have the wedding there in the Spring.

+ + +

On this early spring day, she turned her attention back to the immediate task at hand, of excitedly preparing her wedding dress with Maggie's help, and making quick plans for the event. There was no reason to delay it now that Harvey and she decided to get married. Her sister was buzzing with joy to help plan Jessie's wedding.

Jessie was amazed at the quick turn of events in her life and the chance for happiness again, with love, and maybe still a child. Jessie had thought that all chances of that were behind her.

The thought stirred a brief memory for her, of holding little Edmond protectively from the dangers around him, in a lifeboat on a very dark night. Funny, she hadn't thought of him in quite a while, but the memory made her wonder how he was doing a couple now after their chance meeting.

A few days later, on March 13, 1913, she would soon be Jessie Bortner, and leave Jessie Trout and the two tragedies behind her along with the name, for a new beginning. Getting married and having a new name, would stop all of the eager conversations that her name of Trout, the sinking, and the interviews of her experience led to when she was in Columbus. She was eager to begin her new life with Harvey Bortner.

She marveled at God's hand and healing in her life. He had blessed and restored her life after two tragedies in a year. She felt very thankful and excited again at her future possibilities.

She remembered feeling like her life was over after her first husband's death, and the fact that she would have given up her seat in the lifeboat during the *Titanic* sinking to keep a family together, feeling she had nothing important to live for, and here she was a year later, excited for her wedding day again. With new beginnings less than a year after the sinking, and two years after her first wedding, she smiled in gratitude for this day and her new chapter in life. She was glad and thankful now that she had the chance to be in Lifeboat #9.

+ + +

Jessie and Harvey moved to Tuscola, Michigan, to settle, and bought an 80-acre farm, and a few cattle, and planted crops to feed the family. Harvey's older brother, Killian, moved in to help them run the farm.

Jessie finally had the children she longed for, of her own. On April 14, 1915, she gave birth to Bruce E. Bortner, and she and Harvey delighted in their son. Jessie had another son in 1918, but the baby passed away and she grieved and settled on raising Bruce.

Then, two years later, they had a daughter, Mary Elizabeth, whom they called Betty, on April 20, 1920, and she was so happy to have both a son and a daughter, and her little family. But God had another blessing for her, and Francis Isobel Bortner joined the family on November 8, 1922. Jessie was ecstatic!

Life was a miracle in itself, and Jessie marveled at the second chance at life that she was granted, knowing others never had another chance at life.

She also still had moments of terror when something would set her off, for no apparent reason, and she would fight through it. It mostly had to do with dark, or water, when it happened. Although she longed for the sweet smells and ocean breezes of the Highlands at times, she had no desire to ever sail on a ship again.

Jessie loved her life, tending to the tasks of the farm, and raising her children with Harvey. He worked hard with long hours and days, tending the farm and also working at the General Motors Foundry plant in Flint, and it was nice when they could grab small moments to sit on the porch and catch up on life. He was so loving to her and the kids when he was around. Jessie loved those small moments with him as the day came to a close, listening to the sound of crickets, seeing the flicker of fireflies in the yard, and enjoying the smells of sweet grass and wildflowers, while the kids ran around before bed.

The children were growing up so fast. After Jessie's life ended up so different from what she thought it would be, yet very blessed, she wondered what their futures would hold, and she was excited to see what life had in store for them all.

KELLEY BORTNER

# 11

## Epilogue

*December 30, 1930*

One cold day, at the end of December, the whole family packed up the car to head to a family outing in Flint. It was freezing rain out and Jessie was happy for the blessing that they owned a car now instead of a wagon to travel in the cold. She grabbed some travel blankets in case it was colder later in the night when they returned home and threw them in the backseat of the Buick with the three kids.

She smiled to herself as she got in the front seat next to Harvey, wearing his usual fedora, and thought of how blessed she was for him and her three kids and wondered what the new year, 1931, would hold for them all.

Bruce was fifteen now, and at sixteen Harvey's family members had to leave home and pursue their way in the world. She wondered if Harvey would enforce that with Bruce or let him stay. He was such a big help around the farm when Harvey was working at the Foundry.

Betty was ten years old already with womanhood just around the corner. Jessie remembered that when her sister, Georgina, was twelve, back in Scotland, she had left the house to find work. Looking back now, that age seemed so young.

Young Francis had just turned eight last month and was such a free spirit, she hoped her daughter kept that spirit as she got older.

Harvey was handling the drive in the freezing rain well, and being late December, they were all glad it hadn't been snow today to thwart their outing. As she came out of her thoughts Jessie saw out the window the deep country ditches along the road, many of which were deeper than she was tall. The ditches were filled with black water and ice as night set in, and she felt uneasy.

Jessie felt the familiar, yet unwelcome panic creeping up on her at the sight of the black water in the deep trenches of the ditches that lined the road, and she gripped the door handle and tried to catch her breath. Harvey looked over and recognized the signs of Jessie's panic that came on suddenly at times. Bruce and Betty, in the backseat, were aware of the change in their mother's demeanor as well and were watching her with concern. Francis was singing to herself in the back seat, next to her siblings, unaware at her young age of her mother's distress. In the next instant, the car hit black ice and went into a spin, and in Jessie's panic with her grip on the door handle, she opened the door and jumped out.

TUSCOLA COUNTY ADVERTISER
GUNNEL DISTRICT CORRESPONDENT
Caro, Michigan January 9, 1931

Arbela Woman is Killed in Auto Spill Near Home

Mrs. Harvey Bortner was instantly killed Tuesay afternoon December 30 (1930) 1 1/2 miles south of her home in Arbela when the car in which she was riding left the roadway and turned over. She was pinned beneath the wreckage and death was caused from a broken neck. It is believed that the steering apparatus broke. Several others besides her husband were injured. They were on their way to Flint. Funeral services were held Friday afternoon (January 2, 1931)

Obituary of Jessie Laird Bortner

The car spun around and landed in the ditch, on Jessie, breaking her neck, and she passed instantly at 45 years old. She didn't see 1931, and her last image was of black water.

Bruce, Betty, and Francis recovered from minor injuries and bruises, along with their father. They continued to live at the farm with Harvey, who worked the farm, with his brother, as well as, at the automotive foundry plant.

+ + +

## Years Later

After some years passed, Harvey's brother, Killian, who had helped with the farm all those years, passed away in 1946, and Harvey couldn't work the farm by himself, as he also had a job at the automotive plant, a General Motors Foundry plant in Flint.

Harvey sold the farm and moved his family to a new house nearby. At the time, Betty had two young children, Edna May and Robert Walter, who they called Bob.

When Bob was around 6 years old, Betty married H. Moody, had more children, and raised stepchildren, while the family moved to their own home that they rented while they took care of the cattle for the landlord. Betty's son Bob remembers riding around the farm on a horse led by H. Moody as a very young child. With his stepdad, H. Moody, Bob remembers working the farm chores, cooling off in the pond, and hunting with his coon dogs, which H. Moody had taught him to train.

During this time, Harvey Bortner rented an apartment in town near the plant where he worked. He had a widowed friend in town that he saw, but he never remarried. Harvey would give his grandchildren shiny new coins when he saw them and loved his family.

When Harvey passed away he was buried in Millington, Michigan, in Pine Grove Cemetery, next to Jessie. Jessie's daughter, Betty, purchased a home for her family, along with some land, using her inheritance from Harvey.

Francis and her family lived about a mile from Betty's new home.

Jessie's three sisters, in back row, Mimi, Lottie and Dora.
In front row, her children, Bruce, Francis and Betty.
*Kelley Senkowski / no use without permission*

+ + +

Betty had a sweet, beautiful soul, full of love and grace, and was an exceptional cook. She worked at a local diner part-time, had four children, raised two other stepchildren and adopted one of her grandsons.

Bob enjoyed being the high school football and baseball star and being raised by H. Moody until adulthood. Bob served in the Navy for two years, and after his service, he returned to a job at Eaton Manufacturing Foundry. Then he met and married Jean Elaine Bell in 1964, and his first infant child met H. Moody before his stepfather passed away.

Bob and Jean lived in a house in the city of Saginaw. In 1966, Bob had a wife, toddler and new baby due, and was hired at the local General Motors (GM) plant.

It was in his young adult days that he turned down an offer from a friend to invest in a new franchise, Mcdonald's, that would specialize in hamburgers, and, thinking it was just a burger place that wouldn't get interest from customers, and having a young family to provide for, he stayed at his job with good pay and benefits at GM.

Bob Bortner, Jessie's grandson
*Kelley Senkowski / no use without permission*

When his first couple of kids were very young, Bob brought them to the local ballpark to watch his baseball league games, and even tried out for the Detroit Tigers baseball team, without being selected.

When Jean's parents retired, Bob bought the house in Saginaw Township and moved his family in when his in-laws left to travel around the States. He brought his last baby and wife home from the hospital to their new house where his three kids were waiting with their grandparents to meet their new baby brother.

Bob and Jean raised four children, three daughters, and a son: Robin Jean (4 children); Kelley Elaine (5 children); Karin Lee (3 children); and Robert Walter (Bo). They have twelve grandchildren and seven great-grandchildren, with more to come at the writing of this book.

Bob retired from GM at the age of 55 years and has enjoyed decades of retirement. Bob has always been active enjoying camping, hunting, fishing, golfing, and pickleball.

Kelley, the second of Bob's children, and author of this book, married and had three children and adopted two more sons: Taylor (Christian) Lynne, Austin Kirk, Morgan Elaine, Braydan Robert, and Anthony Gabriel. She divorced after 26 years of marriage, and five years later, in 2022, married a wonderful man, Ken, and now has four more stepchildren of similar age to her children, for a total of nine.

Robert Bortner and daughter, Kelley Bortner
*Kelley Senkowski / no use without permission*

Bruce and Francis's children, their children, grandchildren, and great-grandchildren, as well as the rest of the extended family, are incredibly numerous.

Listed on the next pages are all of the descendants that were born and lived a life...

**All because of Jessie and lifeboat #9.**

# Jessie's Descendants

## Jessie's descendants as of the writing of this book in 2023*

For the sake of the family member's privacy, only first and middle names are listed. Family members are listed by birth order and include a few adoptions into the family, made possible by Jessie's descendants.

*This list is compiled to the best of our extensive research, at the time of writing. Apologies to any family member where there is misinformation or misspelling.*

### HARVEY BORTNER and JESSIE (BRUCE, TROUT)

1. *1915 - 1977* **Bruce** *Edward Bortner*
2. *1918 - 1918 Baby boy*
3. *1920 - 1975 Mary Elizabeth* **(Betty)** *Bortner Moody*
4. *1922 - 1990* **Frances** *Isobol Bortner Hendricks*
5. 1937 Edna Mae (Eddie)
6. 1937 Mona Kay
7. 1939 (Sandy) Bruce Alexander
8. 1941 Maggie McKay
9. 1941 Robert (Bob) Walter
10. 1941 James Newton
11. 1944 Wanda Jane
12. 1945 Sandra Kay
13. 1946 Michael Len
14. 1947 Beverly Jean
15. 1950 Linda Marie
16. 1953 Nola Ann
17. 1957 Douglas Edward
18. 1957 Dean Lee

19. 1959 Danele Renee
20. 1960 Dawn Marie
21. 1960 Kevin Mark
22. 1961 Jean Lee
23. 1961 Stephen Dean
24. 1962 Jack Carl
25. 1962 Molly Kay
26. 1963 Mark Andrew
27. 1963 Dennis James
28. 1964 Barbra J
29. 1964 Robin Jean
30. 1964 David Clayton
31. 1964 Wendy Dawn
32. 1965 Scott Alan
33. 1965 Steven Mark
34. 1966 Kimberly Jean
35. 1966 Kelley Elaine
36. 1967 Kristian K
37. 1967 Daniel James.
38. 1967 Stacey Lynn
39. 1968 Karen Jayne
40. 1968 Catherine
41. 1968 Michael Scott
42. 1969 Karin Lee
43. 1971 Alana Jane
44. 1971 Scot James
45. 1972 Robert (Bo) Walter II
46. 1973 Janette Iris
47. 1973 Todd Russ
48. 1973 Diane F
49. 1973 James Moody
50. 1976 Joshua James
51. 1977 Jacob Thomas
52. 1978 David E
53. 1979 Crystal Lynn
54. 1980 David Paul
55. 1981 Adrian Nicole
56. 1982 Amy Sue

57. 1984 Wesley Mark
58. 1985 James Martin
59. 1985 Jeffery
60. 1986 Joseph Preston
61. 1986 Christine
62. 1987 Cody
63. 1987 Nicholas Andrew
64. 1989 Heather Sue
65. 1989 Alex Michael
66. 1989 Matthew James
67. 1990 Erin Elizabeth
68. 1991 Alexander Dean
69. 1991 Jonathan Mark
70. 1992 William Emmett
71. 1992 Lila Brittany
72. 1992 Jordan
73. 1993 Andrew Daniel
74. 1993 Christopher Robert
75. 1993 Aaron Dean
76. 1994 Taylor (Chris) Lynne
77. 1996 Austin Kirk
78. 1996 Alexander Daniel
79. 1997 Ashlyn Nichole
80. 1999 Morgan Elaine
81. 1999 Emily Marie
82. 2000 Dylan
83. 2000 DeLaney Nicole
84. 2000 Haley
85. 2001 Audrey
86. 2002 Ethan Joe.
87. 2002 Jeremiah Joseph
88. 2002 Abigail (Ashton) A
89. 2003 Ella Jolie
90. 2003 Conner Issac
91. 2003 Braydan Robert
92. 2004 Benjamin David
93. 2006 Kennedy Lane
94. 2006 Anthony Gabriel

95. 2007 Catherine Angela
96. 2008 Colin Victor
97. 2009 Maddox Jack
98. 2010 Aiden McCoy
99. 2012 Olivia Grace
100. 2013 Stella Frances
101. 2015 Carter Allen
102. 2016 Avery James
103. 2017 Emmiline Pate
104. 2017 Quinn Maydell
105. 2017 Sabastian William
106. 2017 Maximus Wesley
107. 2019 Parker Michelle
108. 2019 Piper Jean
109. 2019 Maverick William
110. 2019 Blake Carolina
111. 2020 Braxton Duane
112. 2020 Adelynn Blaine
113. 2021 Wilder Mark
114. 2021 Jayson Dean
115. 2022 William (Liam) Emmett
116. 2022 Kyzen Christopher
117. 2022 Oaklee Mae
118. 2023 Riley Dean
119. 2023 Parker Grey
120. 2023 Baby R
121. ...

# RELATIVES DIDN'T KNOW MRS. TROUT ON TITANIC 'TIL SHE ARRIVED HERE

Columbus, Monday Apr 22

# The

In Her Own Words

**FOURTEENTH YEAR.**

Telephone your WA
ADS, to Bell 640
Citizen 2905.

# FRANKLIN ADM
# WRECK SIX HO

Vice President of White Star L

Responsibility For Cruel H

Big Liner and All On Boar

MRS. JESSIE TROUT.

## RECOVER 50 BO

By United Press.

NEW YORK, April 22.—Fifty bodies
times were recovered by the cable ship M
cording to the following message received
offices here today by wireless:

"Latitudes 41.58, longitude 49.21—heav
has interfered with operations. Fifty bod
not embalmed. Will be buried at sea 8 p. m.
Can only bring embalmed bodies to port."

The message was dated Sunday, an
number of bodies of the Titanic victims have
mitted to the deep from the morgue ship.

By United Press.

WASHINGTON, April 22.—Over
six hours before the news was made
public, the White Star line knew 20
lifeboats filled with passengers of
the Titanic had been picked up by
the Carpathia. This was admitted
today by Vice President P. A. S.
Franklin of the International Mer-
cantile Marine company, the first
witness today before the senate in-
vestigating committee.

At noon last Monday this was
known. Franklin said, but it was
not made public "because it was
not authentic." Not until 6:20 last

This informa
"mere rumo
give it out j
could not be
sunk," and s
thentic infor

At 6:20 th
came with th
disaster." T
then, was the

DISCI

Admitting
of the Whit
out the cruel
that the Thi
all safe, Vice
the line toda

Mrs. Jessie Trout, widow of W.
N. Trout, a Scioto Valley switchman who was accidentally killed
last September at the Mound street

vented the separation of any
husband and wife or brother
and sister. Since the tragic
death of my husband here last
September, life has not been
to me what it was before.

## Father, Mother and Babe All Saved in Separate Lifeboats

Miss Helen Newsome who, with her parents, Mr. and Mrs.
Richard L. Beckwith, was taken from the Titanic in the second lifeboat that left her, was responsible for the bringing about of a tearful
and happy reunion on board the Carpathia of a father, mother and
baby, all of whom left the Titanic in different boats and after both
parents had given the other members of the family up for lost, according to Perrin B. Monypeny, who met the Beckwiths when the
Carpathia landed in New York.

As the lifeboat in which Beckwiths left the Titanic was being
lowered over the side Miss Newsome, who was seated near the middle of the boat, felt a soft bundle drop into her lap and unfolding
the blanket in which it was wrapped found that it was a baby. She
cared for it during the hours that the occupants of the lifeboat
waited for the aid brought by the Carpathia, and after several hours
on board the latter liner located its parents, who had themselves
only discovered that the other had been saved but a few moments
before.

According to Mr. Monypeny, the Beckwiths would not have left
the Titanic at all had not Mrs. Beckwith insisted on doing so in spite
of her husband's declaration that it "was foolish to leave the ship."
Upon Mrs. Beckwith's insistence, Mr. Beckwith finally went below
and, seeing that the whole hold and the lower part of the ship was
filled with water, agreed to leave to be on the safe side. Until after
he left the ship and saw her gradually sink he, like many other passengers that were lost, did not believe that it was possible for the
Titanic to sink.

# TEN DROWNED WHEN VESSELS CRASH IN FOG

**Special to The Citizen.**

GALVESTON, TEX., April 22.—
The freight steamer El Sud of the
Southern Pacific line and the passenger boat Denver of the Mallory
line crashed together in a dense fog
late last night off Galveston bar. Ten
lives were lost, those of deckhands
who were knocked overboard. One
deckhand of the El Sud was badly
hurt.

The crash occurred 15 miles from
Bolivar light. For a time it was
feared that El Sud would sink.
Down at the bow, the El Sud raced
for the shore and was beached on
Galveston bar. She was saved from
sinking by her forward bulkhead
having withstood the inrush of the
sea as the bow plates were ripped
off.

There were 100 passengers on
the Denver and a crew of 70. There
was a wild rush for life preservers
and the lifeboats of the Denver
after the crash, but Captain Charles
P. Staples and First Officer Lamb

## SAYS OWNERS ARE TO BLAME FOR DISASTER

**By United Press.**

NEWARK, N. J., April 22.—"Do
not blame this tragedy on God;
blame it on the owners who took all
these chances for the sake of gain,"
declared Rev. Henry R. Rose, pastor of the Church of the Redeemer,
in a sermon upon the Titanic disaster.

"Do not blame the captain. He
was employed and had to obey the
orders of the superior who was
aboard, the man who rode away on
a lifeboat and left the captain to
die and 1600 souls to their fate, a
fate that he, with others, were
guilty before God for helping to cre-
ate."

## HANGED HIMSELF IN FUN; ALMOST DIED

**Special to The Citizen.**

SPRINGFIELD, O., April 22.—
"Want to see how people get
hanged?" asked Paul Simmons,
11, of Earnest Harmon, 5. "Sure,"
answered Ernest.

Paul tied a rope to the limb of
a tree, placed the noose about his
neck and swung off. Ernest, thinking he was playing, left him struggling violently to free himself.

In the house a half-hour later
Ernest "wondered if Paul got
hung." His parents rushed out

109

Bell and D. B. Horn, also charged
with breaking the speed law, were
each fined $25 and costs.

# DIDN'T KNOW MRS. TROUT ON TITANIC 'TIL SHE ARRIVED

(Continued From Page One.)

him on the Titanic and he was very
devoted to them. There was no
mother with them. I had the
youngest in my care. The other
child was in another lifeboat.

"We were probably half a mile
from the Titanic when she went
down. It was a terrible sight. Not
until 7 o'clock in the morning were
we picked up by the Carpathia,
although lightly dressed, seemed to
stand it better than the men. The
women also seemed more composed
on the Titanic than the men.

"I was traveling alone and had
made friends on the boat with Miss
Marian Wright, who was going to
Portland, Ore., to be married, and
Mrs. Watt and her daughter, who
were gong to join Mrs. Watt's husband in Portland, Ore. They were
all saved.

"On Sunday night before the boat
sank we had services in the dining
room of the second cabin, and a
Rev. Mr. Carter of the Whitechapel
district in London, who was on his
way to Kansas City to visit a brother, led us in prayer for the safe arrival of the ship."

## HELPED IN NEW YORK.

Mrs. Trout said she was supplied
with clothing and $25 in New
York to come to Columbus. The
only thing she saved was her night
clothes, a coat, a handbag, her
bracelet and back comb. In her
handbag she had her check book.

Mrs. Trout was born in Scotland
and came to this country seven
years ago with her parents, Mr.
and Mrs. George Bruce, who lived
until recently on the Johnson farm,
near Camp Chase. She was married
March 28, 1911, to W. H. Trout, a
switchman employed in the Hock-
ing Valley yards. Seven months
later on the night of Sept. 22, 1911,
he was ground to death under a
cut of cars.

Grief-stricken, Mrs. Trout went
back to Scotland to visit her grand-
mother and sisters to recover from
the shock of her husband's death.
She and her husband had lived at
1264 ½ West Broad street.

# VETERAN HARNESS MAKER IS CALLED

Robert Sartain, aged 80, father
of Sheriff Albert Sartain, died at
his home, 809 Beech street, Monday
morning from the infirmities of age.
He is survived by six children—
Sheriff Sartain, William H. Sartain,

## "THE GREATEST KIDNEY REMEDY ON EARTH," SAYS A GRATEFUL WOMAN

I want to tell you how much good
your Swamp-Root did me. About
four years ago I suffered from what
the doctors called fistula and for two
years of that time, I endured what
no tongue can tell. I also had in-
flammation of the bladder and I tried
doctors' medicines without receiving
any help. Someone told me about Dr.
Kilmer's Swamp-Root.

After giving it a thorough trial, I
received relief, so kept on using it
and today I am a strong and well woman. If I ever feel badly or out of
sorts, I take Swamp-Root and it always straightens me out. I honestly
believe that this medicine would cure
all troubles you recommend it for
and it is a pleasure for me to send
my testimony and photograph to
you. I think Dr. Kilmer's Swamp-
Root is one of the greatest medicines on earth.

Respectfully yours,
MRS. JOHN BAILEY,
Portland, Ind.

Subscribed and sworn to before me
this 12th day of July, 1909.
C. A. BENNETT,
Notary Public.

Letter to
Dr. Kilmer & Co.,
Binghamton, N. Y.

Prove What Swamp-Root Will Do
For You

Send to Dr. Kilmer & Co., Binghamton, N. Y., for a sample bottle. It
will convince anyone. You will also
receive a booklet of valuable information, telling all about the kidneys
and bladder. When writing, be sure
and mention Dept N. Regular fifty-
cent and one-dollar size bottles for
sale at all drug stores.

# Acknowledgements

I want to take a moment to thank many people for their support and assistance in the journey to tell Jessie's story. I also am grateful to my Father in heaven, for giving me the story with the facts at hand, so I did not need to invent it.

- Thank you to my sister, Robin, for her partnership on all of the research. Her research in the late 1990s in talking to Jessie's remaining siblings at the time, locating articles, and her time finding documentation such as birth, death, and immigration records were instrumental for the story flow. This was an amazing help to me in putting together the many pieces of Jessie's life journey.
- Thank you to my daughter, Morgan for her edits and for motivating me to do all of the edits needed. Also, to the couple of friends who read the drafts and offered feedback.
- A special thank you to Curt Harding for his many recommendations on the publishing and design of the book, in an industry that was foreign to me at the start.
- A heartfelt thank you to my husband, family, and friends, for all of the encouragement and support over the years for motivation to pursue the dream of telling Jessie's story, so it is not lost to history. This is for, and represents, all of my family members - those already gone, those here now, and those to come, who are here because of Jessie and Lifeboat #9.

# About Titanic Resources

There are a variety of places to look for more information on the R.M.S Titanic, the sinking, and the survivor list. Here are some thoughts and recommendations on Titanic resources.

### Websites

With the internet at your fingertips, there is a plethora of resources from which to choose. As with information on the internet, one needs to research where it is coming from and that it is fact-based. Some websites you might want to check are Wikipedia for the survivor list and passenger information, National Geographic and the Britannica websites for facts, as well as other researched websites. www.TitanicQuest.com is a resource for information on Jessie's Titanic experience.

You can find documentation of births, deaths or immigration on ancestry websites or public records of the city where the document was listed. Many are online, but some very old ones may be archived and you would need to request them.

### Images

Many images that you see on public websites online of the Titanic are now considered public use/domain, due to the images being over 100 years old. However, before using, always check the Creative Commons license to ensure that you do not need a license or permission to use an image.

### Books

There are currently several, well-researched books available with facts of the Titanic tragedy, yet few offer the story as told by the survivor, so these are a rare find. Enjoy them.

I believe this is due in part to the era in which the tragedy happened. It was a time without social media or television. Book writing was rare and reserved for the affluent, or those in academia, with the means to afford it, so books were harder to come by than they are today. Printing multiple copies in that era was also difficult and cumbersome for circulating writings.

In addition, the culture at that time was not one of sharing life's details to all within hearing distance and much was not talked about, or processed emotionally in a way that led to healing of trauma, so the traumatic detailed accounts were hard to come by.

Although, there are many books, one that I have found offers a place that summarizes information well from other writings in one place is, Titanic: An Illustrated History, by Don Lynch, yet there are many books offered on the sinking.

Printed in the USA
CPSIA information can be obtained
at www.ICGtesting.com
LVHW051917221223
767229LV00010B/179

9 781088 045466